Human Existence as Radical Reality

Ortega y Gasset's Philosophy of Subjectivity

Human Existence as Radical Reality

Ortega y Gasset's Philosophy of Subjectivity

Pedro Blas Gonzalez

First Edition 2005

Published in the United States by
Paragon House
2285 University Avenue West
St. Paul, MN 55114

    Cover photo by Giselle Freund, 1938

Library of Congress Cataloging-in-Publication Data

Gonzalez, Pedro Blas, 1964-
    Human existence as radical reality : Ortega y Gasset's philosophy of subjectivity/
    by Pedro Blas Gonzalez.-- 1st ed.
        p. cm.
    Includes bibliographical references.
    ISBN-13: 978-1-55778-840-5 (pbk. : alk. paper)
1. Ortega y Gasset, Jose, 1883-1955. I. Title.

    B4568.O74G57 2005
    196'.1--dc22

                        2004026565

    The paper used in this publication meets the minimum requirements of Amer-
    ican National Standard for Information Sciences—Permanence of Paper for
    Printed Library Materials, ANSIZ39.48-1984.

Manufactured in the United States of America
10 9 8 7 6 5 4 3 2 1

    For current information about all releases from Paragon House,
        visit the web site at http://www.paragonhouse.com

Para mis padres, Pedro y Nelida, que me enseñaron el arte de vivir y pensar.

To my wife, Anne, and my children, Isabella Sophia and Marcus Julian, for being witnesses to my life.

CONTENTS

Preface

Ortega y Gasset's Vital Philosophical Innovation

On first encountering José Ortega y Gasset's (1883–1955) work by way of the Spanish philosophers Miguel de Unamuno and Julian Marias, the latter of whom was a student of Ortega's in a movement that has come to be known as the school of Madrid, I developed an affinity for his philosophy that has ever since taken deep root within the structure of my thought. At first I became attracted to Ortega's work through his first book, *Meditaciónes del Quijote (Meditations on Quixote)*, published in 1914.[1] But this fact in itself is hardly of any importance because *Meditations* has often served as the port of entry, as it were, for so many other thinkers on first discovering Ortega's work.

It was his metaphysical depiction of the forest of El Escorial in the opening pages of that work that first captured my imagination. I was moved by his description of the denseness of the forest. However, I knew that a detailed cataloging of the natural world was not what this work was about; therefore I continued to read in anticipation. In essence, his description of the rankness and vastness of the forest is a perfect introduction to his thought for any newcomer to his phenomenological manner of thinking. There can be no mistake as to Ortega's overall phenomenological project in *Meditations*. Very early in this work Ortega leads one to believe that something other than a poetic rendition of vegetation and foliage is at issue. With every glance that the author offered of the endless array of trees in the woods, I began to view the woods as a metaphysical labyrinth that was no bigger and no more perplexing than man's own existential condition. Now, I know that the word "existential" has attained a perhaps too popular and ominous reputation, especially in contexts where the word is little understood, but this truism need not always be the case.

Existential concerns have always been those human concerns that are embraced by our own self-conscious subjectivity. Thus only from such self-awareness of our subjectivity can a vital individuality flow.

The forest that surrounds the monastery of El Escorial and which Ortega finds himself amidst is never experienced as the totality of a forest. The Monasterio de San Lorenzo de el Escorial is today the site of one of Spain's greatest art collections. It is situated forty-nine kilometers from Madrid and is bordered by the Sierra de Guardarrama and the village of San Lorenzo del Escorial. Ortega found this site a personal oasis because the forest represented the openness and vastness of human experience for him. The forest symbolizes the entirety of the universe as an objectifying force of which we only share in as subjects, and this, through our personal self-conscious perspective. Thus, this woodland is never to be simply equated with the spatial-temporal totality where I find myself. The reason for this is because the forest is always breaking up into a series of "angles" that overlap and which my consciousness can only entertain in isolation. The forest, then, is to reality what the handful of trees in my vicinity is to my perspective. Therefore any particular locale in which I may subsequently find myself in the woods becomes the center of the universe—the center of reality proper. The individual trees themselves are therefore the culprits of my not seeing the entire forest. Hence at first glance the forest appears only as an otherwise incoherent conglomeration of towering oaks and ashes. Here, the trees create a blanket over the sky that keeps out all but the most indirect and stubborn slivers of sunlight.

And as is also well expected, the silence here is perennial—primeval will perhaps serve as a more accurate description. Any wayward visitor to such a place quickly finds himself as an alien in his own company. In such a site we can hear the blood rushing through our temples. But this is precisely the authentic and thus confrontational character of solitude, which enables us to hear our own pulsating heart beating. When finding ourselves in this threatening circumstance, there can be no other recourse but to face this silence and embrace our immediate consciousness of ourselves—serving as an exaltation of our existence.

Hence these were my very first crude and unsophisticated impressions of Ortega's portrayal of subjectivity; the individual struggling to gain equal footing with material reality. And from my deciphering of his eloquent sentences, I came to the realization that the forest is indeed synonymous with human existence—a totality that is in search of the necessary coherence that will enable it from slipping into an alien and sterile objectivity. With this realization I began to understand that it is the lack of exercising our individual self-consciousness that is often the main obstacle in man's truly arriving at a self-understanding of what Ortega refers to as radical reality. Reality, Ortega argues throughout this work, is absolute and objective, but our finite and thus limited perspective keeps us from visualizing its overall design and coherence. But this kind of exhaustive rendition of truth, he suggests, is best left to the omniscience of God anyhow. However, reality, he reasons, is always perspectival. Thus Ortega launches his philosophy with an eye toward the questioning of the nature of appearance and reality. The work of the thinker, he tells us, is to attempt to piece together, to find coherence in what is otherwise a series of vague impressions. Ortega is using the word meditation in the same sense that the ancient stoics like Marcus Aurelius thought of it. The nature of meditation is unlike that of theory, hypothesis, and scientific experimentation. A meditation, then, is truly no other than a genuine Socratic elenchus, where the knower is a seeker after truth. In many respects the essayistic qualities of *Meditaciónes del Quijote* can be compared to Alain's *The Gods,* through its portrayal of ultimate questions with the pressing seriousness that such concerns have for a vital existence.

This explains the title of his majestic book, *Meditations on Quixote.* Yet we must keep in mind that Cervantes' portrayal of Don Quijote is not exactly a work about a character who is mentally deranged. This would be an all-too-literal and simplistic reading of a work that is considered by many to be the first novel.[2] The errant and gallivanting Don Quijote de la Mancha along with his sidekick Sancho Panza is really best said to be searching after an ideal vision of reality. *Don Quijote* is more akin to the philosophical description of the way of opinion and the way of truth as rendered by the Greek thinker Parmenides than he is to any one-dimensional portrayal of insanity.[3] I find it significant that such a comic work should be one of the most surefooted attempts to answer such perplexing human conundrums, as is for instance the nature of appearance and reality. Ortega argues that Cervantes was interested in the portrayal of a character that finds himself with the vital need to search for the fine points of the nature of appearance and reality. This is significant because to become enmeshed in such a metaphysical search is precisely what the philosophical life ought to be about. But this is additionally important because the metaphysical orientation and temperament of such a person is what drives any genuine drive to understand reality. The ancient problem of appearance and reality is the vital task that Ortega attributes to Don Quijote. Thus, this work—this *Meditations on Quixote,* is not just a work of literary criticism, but also rather the positing of a metaphysical problem. But this *Quijotismo,* as Ortega refers to Don Quijote's search, is a vital concern, Ortega tells us. Metaphysics, then, is none other than a perpetual and vitally existential situating of man in the cosmos. Hence, that Ortega should begin this phenomenological investigation with the example of Don Quijote de la Mancha as the epitome of the search for truth is not a coincidence. As Don Quijote so eloquently alludes to, this philosophical endeavor is also a solitary task. What makes this enterprise a lonely one is the fact that what is fundamentally at stake is not necessarily ideas, but our salvation as individuals. The essential difference between Ortega's, "I am I and my circumstances" and Don Quijote's courageous trek out into the world is simply a desire—an inquietude, let us say, that cannot conform itself with the apparent nature and status quo of appearance.

Man, Ortega informs us, is a metaphysically problematic

entity who must bargain for either seeing the obverse or reverse of his life at any given time, but who is also such a being that does not have the luxury of focusing on both simultaneously. Thus, Ortega appropriately enough refers to his first book as being a kind of meditation. A meditation is what a long time ago thinkers would engage in order to peel off the often-irresolute layers of reality.[4] A meditation has as its central core the understanding that many surprises may be in store for he who reflects. And yet a meditation is a reflective process, and not necessarily a prescriptive end. Hence to meditate is a sincere search for the nature of truth. Unlike theorizing, where the results are often found in advance and merely made to pass muster, meditation is instead pure reflection. The always-hoped-for result of a meditation is that of wisdom, that is, the underlying first principles that give unity to our understanding of reality.

Hence, I found such very real existential concerns in Ortega's work to be utterly refreshing, especially in this epoch of pseudo-analytic philosophical problems. It seems to me that the greatest fact that man must contend with—thinkers and nonphilosophers alike, is our vital awareness of existence itself and not the many varied and dispersed facts that make up the material circumstances of biological life. Of course, I began to view Ortega as partaking in my overall concerns as well as sharing in my temperament. After realizing that every philosopher entertains problems in equal proportion to his vocation and temperament, as Schilling and Ortega have emphasized, I knew then that a further sustained and in-depth reading of his work was in order.

The striking phenomenon of Ortega's description of the forest of El Escorial is that he is making a statement about the very essence of what it means to be human on the one hand, and what it might mean to philosophize on the other. He begins the work by posing the not-so-rhetorical question: How many trees does it take to make a forest? The import of such a question is that Ortega is truly wondering how best to appropriate the nature of human existence. Most people demand of reality that it manifest itself the same as all other superficial things, Ortega tells us. But seeing that the more profound aspects of reality do not readily manifest themselves as ready-made to the multitude, the many begin to turn their back on the question of truth altogether, often out of a sheer lack of wonder. Hence, the project of truth is abandoned due to a loss of will, a maddening boredom that chokes its adherents.

The forest acts as a kind of metaphorical primordial land where we find ourselves in existential solitude for the first time. But this is not a palatable situation at first, Ortega reminds us. The main reason for this being that the resistance that the world offers me also allows me to discover my vocation. But the greatest contribution that Ortega makes to the discipline of philosophy is his more often than not implicit challenge to modern philosophers to return their attention to reflecting on the nature of philosophy as a vocation. Philosophy, he insists, must remain a vital possibility for man. Philosophy must be practiced as a way of life. Ortega was totally against the mania for neologism that modernity has so aptly exhibited. He and other thinkers like Kierkegaard, Unamuno, Gabriel Marcel, and Camus were horrified by what had become of philosophical vocation. But vocation and a true desire for wisdom is precisely what are missing from philosophy today. Yet, how does one say this and remain with the illusion that the very people that one is addressing will even have a ghost of a chance to make sense of this contention? Philosophical vocation, then, is what guides and inspires the thinker in his daily, very often mundane life, even through trivial affairs. Thus, philosophy as a vital way of life is often a reticent reminder to the thinker that reason and life are dual aspects of the same phenomenon. Ortega was a thinker of old—one who saw through the "things of the world" with the poetic sensitivity that is so central to philosophical vision.

Philosophical reflection attempts to unify—to paste together a world, a reality that is never ready-made. The thinker puts together the pieces of a tapestry that can only have genuine meaning in their totality. But isn't this also the work of the scientist, someone may ask? Perhaps this is true as well of the scientist, with the major exception that throughout this dialectical process the thinker finds himself existentially in the center of this dilemma. This existential conundrum is always with me, regardless of what I do or where I may find myself. Man is said to be a transnatural subjectivity that always finds himself at the center of the universe. Philosophy, taken in the right way, that is, for one's individual salvation, as Alain (Emile-Auguste Chartier, 1868–1951) has so beautifully defined it, can only enlighten us.[5]

Thus, having studied all of Ortega's major writings, I began to see the shortcomings, ambiguities, and paradoxes that are so commonplace in every attempt at thinking on such a large scale. Hence this essay is not only a sympathetic portrayal of the main themes and their respective inconsistencies found in Ortega's work. I have learned a great deal from Ortega about thinking proper. I have done this by allowing his work to sharpen my own thought with his brilliant allegorical and metaphorical exigencies. Perhaps his greatest lesson is that philosophical rigor does not have to be pedantic. Erudition and pedantry ought not to be confused one with the other. Erudition enlightens while pedantry merely obfuscates. Ortega often stressed his conviction that clarity is the courtesy that the thinker owes the reader. For this reason, those who knew Ortega personally, as Octavio Paz, assert that his writings were an extension of his conversations.[6]

Therefore, in concluding I must say that the only proper justification for this essay is to be found in my attempt to bring some of Ortega's concerns into the mainstream of current philosophical dialogue, where I believe they may be justly served. Also, I find it very important that Ortega's work be reintroduced to a new generation. His work is very appropriate to an understanding of life today when more than ever before human life seems to be increasingly lived with a devastating negation of the subjective. A conviction that one is not willing to live out is only a theory. Thus in this regard, Ortega teaches us that we find ourselves surrounded by silence in embarking in this all too challenging terra incognita that is better known as subjective existence.

Introduction

This work is a critical study of José Ortega y Gasset's attempt to reconcile his notion of lived experience (life as radical reality), which is immediate experience, with his idea of life as vital-reason. Life as vital-reason is best understood as consisting of life as a rational-existential project. This in effect is Ortega's manner of fusing idealism and realism. This union results in the self-with-things or what amounts to I-in-the-world. In Ortega's thought, man is never what he is in his immediacy, and therefore he must create his essence through a self-conscious existential project.

This existential project is an attempt to reclaim the importance of an awareness of the immediacy that is individual human life as subjectivity. Thus, Ortega's notion of life as radical reality is the culmination of an underlying dialectic that is found throughout his work. But man's self-awareness of his life as both, a prereflective as well as an extranatural cosmic phenomenon, Ortega argues, is forcibly manifested through a confrontation with the material world.

This vital clash necessitates an inward glance where the self discovers its subjectivity. Therefore, I conclude this work by asserting that for Ortega, the synthesis of these apparently antithetical notions culminates in a form of subjective vitalism, given that primacy is necessarily attributed to the self over the external world. The focus of this work, then, concerns the fundamental tenet of Ortega's argument concerning the synthesis of realism and idealism; and rationalism and vitalism, as well as the inherent existential tension that exists in this endeavor. Given Ortega's notion that all thought must originate and therefore concern itself with life as phenomenon, his philosophy necessarily gives primacy to the self over the material world. "*Yo soy yo y mis circumstancias*" ("I am I and my circumstances") stresses the nature of the rational vitalism that results from this self-awareness of life as a problem for reflection, which is forged from man's necessary encounter with the world. The result of this self-knowledge is the foundation of a metaphysics of life that is best understood as man as radical reality. Ortega argues that all philosophical problems always recoil into questions of individual life. Ortega's notion "I am I and my circumstances" is also very much the same theme that Camus develops in *The Myth of Sisyphus*. The main difference found in these two thinkers, however, is that what Camus refers to as "the absurd," Ortega simply sees as being beyond the rational grasp of man, and thus as neither absurd nor meaningful. Ortega's notion of man is one of a cosmic being that is forced to make sense of his local situation, thus his individual circumstance.

This work traces Ortega's intellectual development from his early neo-Kantian influence while a student in Marburg under the tutelage of Hermann Cohen and Paul Natorp, and leading up to his notion of life as biographical narrative. Close attention is paid to what can be referred to as Ortega's humanistic approach to philosophical reflection. Undoubtedly, Ortega's work stresses the plight of subjectivity, as this attempts to realize itself as a conscious entity in the universe. As such, Ortega's work can be called a metaphysics of subjectivity. The parallels between his early work and that of life-philosophy are emphasized. Also, the existentialist themes in his thought are explored in relation to the work of other existentialists.

Also, it is important to say a few words about Ortega's writing style. Ortega was a master of the most French of all genres: the essay. He is considered a great essayist and stylist of the Spanish language. A large number of his articles first appeared in newspapers. He had the firm conviction that the newspaper format should enlighten and educate as well as inform the general public. Besides being a very noble idea, this also forced Ortega to write in a manner that kept rigorous philosophical reflection as a viable option for a discerning public. However, upon saying that I caution that this is a true aid to the clarity of his work and a genuine service to the discipline of philosophy. Nowhere has it been established, much less proven, that philosophical works should be abstruse treatises written by myopic academics. Where his thought is rigorous and engrossing, his language is often simple and clear. And where, more often than not, his essayistic instinct is searching and awe-inspiring, his guidance as a thinker clears the way with analogy.

The book is divided into eight chapters. The preface introduces and guides the reader to some of the main topics and themes that are found in Ortega's work. Also, in an effort to help locate the trajectory of Ortega's life and thought, I have offered a chronology of the major professional events and the dates of publication of his major works. This can become a very worthwhile tool when a comparison of Ortega's works is necessary in light of the thought of other thinkers. Chapter 1 traces Ortega's early neo-Kantian influence while a student at Marburg under the tutelage of Hermann Cohen and Paul Natorp. Chapter 2 continues from the influence of his first major published article, "Adam in Paradise," to questions of human existence in lieu of the phenomenological method. In chapter 3, I introduce the clash that Ortega saw between pure reason and vital beliefs. The nature of beliefs is an essential aspect of Ortega's work. Also, I would add that Ortega was very prophetic in seeing the rise of a tired and seemingly directionless excess of intellectual verbiage. For this reason he said that he did not bother to read professional philosophy journals. He was of the conviction that no genuine philosophy could be found in such publications.

Chapter 4 traces the importance of the existential categories in Ortega's work. This chapter takes subjectivity in isolation and thus serves as a clarification of themes that have to do with man and society later on. In chapter 5, the nature of social relationships is developed. Ortega is adamant in stressing that man is a social entity that not only needs to take part in society, but also that in doing so confronts his own subjective nature. Chapter 6 takes up the political dimension of man. Ortega's classic book, *The Revolt of the Masses,* takes a closer look at the problems of a genuine subjectivity vis-à-vis objectifying forces. This chapter explores the practical and very pressing issues that Ortega viewed as being central to both existential conditions: *alteración* and *ensimismamiento.*

In chapter 7, Ortega's "biographical life" is compared with what the French writer Paul Valery has called a "conscious calculation." This comparison allows for a broader showcasing of Ortega's major philosophical concerns and inquietudes. I do compare Ortega's work with other of his contemporaries, but a comparison with Valery shows the proximity that exists between the poetic sensibility and philosophical rigor. Chapter 8 also looks closely at Ortega's later existentialist themes as well as offers an argument that posits where Ortega may have anticipated the thought of Sartre. Last, the book contains a glossary of Ortega's more recurrent terminology. I believe that this will help the reader to clarify what Ortega means by the terms that he employs.

Chronology

1883

On May 9, José Ortega y Gasset is born in Madrid, Spain.

1891–97

Ortega attends a Jesuit school in Malaga in the province of Andalusia.

1898

Ortega begins to study philosophy at the University of Madrid.

1902

Ortega publishes *Glosas*, and thus begins his objectivist period that does not end until 1914.

1904

Ortega receives his doctorate in philosophy from the University of Madrid. His thesis is titled "The Terrors of Year One Thousand," an analysis of French medieval history.

1905

Ortega departs for Germany. From April to November he studies at the University of Leipzig where he becomes acquainted with the work of Nietzsche, Schopenhauer, Humboldt, and Darwin. He studies with Wilhelm Wundt.

1906

Ortega enrolls at the University of Marburg and studies with Paul Natorp and Hermann Cohen. Here he is introduced to neo-Kantianism.

1908

Ortega founds the newspaper *Faro*. He also begins to teach logic, ethics, and psychology at La Escuela Superior de Magisterio, a faculty of education.

1910

Ortega is wed to Rosa Spottorno Topete. He founds *Europa*. He is appointed professor of metaphysics at the University of Madrid. He publishes "*Adan en el Paraíso*" ("Adam in Paradise").

1911

Ortega begins to study the works of Max Scheler and is subsequently influenced by Scheler's philosophical anthropology. At this time he is also introduced to Husserl's phenomenology, which at first Ortega welcomes as a useful tool that could be used as a bridge between his neo-Kantian schooling and his developing and preliminary notion of vital-reason.

1914

Ortega publishes *Vieja y Nueva Política; Meditaciónes del Quijote*. In *Meditations on Quixote*, Ortega writes about his concern with the theme of appearance and reality. This was to be a three-volume work, but volumes 2 and 3 were never written. End of his objectivist period and the beginning of his perspectivist period that runs until 1923.

1915

Ortega founds the newspaper *España*.

1916

Ortega publishes the first installment of *El Espectador I* and *Personal, Obras, Cosas*.

1917

El Espectador II and *III* are published.

1921

España Invertebrada (Invertebrate Spain); Bosquejo de Algunos Pensamientos Históricos are published.

1922

El Tema de Nuestro Tiempo (The Modern Theme) is published.

1923

Ortega publishes *El Sentido Histórico de la Teoria de Einstein; Las Atlantidas*.

1924

La Deshumanización del Arte (The Dehumanization of Art); Ideas Sobre La Novela (Ideas about the Novel), and *Ni Vitalismo ni Racionalismo (Neither Vitalism nor Rationalism)* are published. The beginning of Ortega's ratio-vitalist period.

1926

Estudios Sobre el Amor (Studies on Love) is published.

1928

Notas, which eventually is translated as *Notes on Thinking,* is published.

1929

What Is Philosophy? is first delivered as a lecture. *La Rebelión de las Masas (The Revolt of the Masses)* is published. Ortega begins to study Dilthey in depth, even though he was already familiar with him, dating back to the beginning of the century.

1930

Misión de la Universidad (Mission of the University) is published.

1933

Goethe Desde Dentro (Goethe from Within) is published.

1939

Ensimismamiento y Alteración; Meditación de la Tecnica (Meditations on Technology) are published.

1940

"Ideas y Creencias" ("Ideas and Beliefs") is published.

1941

História Como Sistema y del Imperio Romano (History as a System) is published.

1948

Ortega and Julian Marias, one of his "disciples," found the Instituto de Humanidades. Here Ortega reads "An Interpretation of Universal History."

1949

Ortega lectures in Aspen, Colorado, as part of the Goethe bicentennial celebration.

1950

Papeles Sobre Velázquez y Goya (Papers on Velázquez).

1951

Ortega is awarded an honorary doctorate at the University of Glasgow.

1955

In May, Ortega lectures in Venice, Italy. On October 18, Ortega dies of stomach cancer at home in his Madrid apartment in the company of his family.

1957

El Hombre y La Gente (Man and People) and *Que Es Filosofiá? (What Is Philosophy?)* are published.

1958

La Idea de Principio en Leibniz y la Evolución de la Teoría Deductiva (The Idea of Principle in Leibniz and the Evolution of Deductive Theory); Idea del Teatro (Idea of the Theater) Meditación del Pueblo Joven; Prólogo Para Alemanes (Preface for Germans) are published.

1960

Una Interpretación de la Historia Universal (An Interpretation of Universal History); En Torno a Toynbee; Meditación de Europa (Meditation on Europe); Origin y Epílogo de la Filosofiá (Origin of Philosophy) are published.

1961

Vives-Goethe is published.

1962

Pasado y Porvenir Para el Hombre Actual is published.

1966

Unas Lecciónes de Metafísica (Some Lessons on Metaphysics) is published.

1979

Sobre La Razón Histórica (Historical Reason) is published.

1998

"Medio Siglo de Filosofiá" ("Half a Century of Philosophy") is translated into English in *Philosophy Today*. In this latter work, an analysis of philosophy from 1900–1950, Ortega argues that only through the genre of biography can the true form of historical reason be understood.

Chapter One

Part I The Neo-Kantian Background of Ortega's Thought

> I found myself in the beginning then, with this basic two-fold discovery: that one's own life is the fundamental reality and that life is circumstantial. Each of us exists as a castaway in his circumstances, and it is there, whether he wishes or not, that man must struggle to remain afloat.
>
> —*Phenomenology and Art*, p. 57

The intellectual reservoir from which José Ortega y Gasset grounded his thinking is undoubtedly found in great part in the influence that the thought of Hermann Cohen and Paul Natorp exerted over the young Spaniard while he was a student at Marburg. In 1904, after receiving his doctoral degree from the University of Madrid, Ortega began his illustrious career as a journalist by writing for the daily newspaper *El Imparcial*. In 1905 he left Spain for Germany, where he studied at the universities of Leipzig and Berlin.[1] However, it was during his stay at Marburg (1906–1908) that Ortega began to reflect upon his own circumstances as a Spaniard and a European, which would later prove to be such a central issue in his thinking.

It was also at Marburg that Ortega developed the stoic attitude toward human life that eventually became the central idea behind his belief that "I am I and my circumstances." In other words, Marburg removed Ortega from the "matter of fact" pragmatism of Spanish life. During this early period, Ortega begins to view life as something that must be justified and not just merely lived. Thus, life for him now began to weigh down on him with an existential vigor that required contemplation and deliberation in order to "save our circumstances."[2] That is, life is not complete in itself until one creates it in one's image. He explains:

> Man reaches his full capacity when he acquires complete
> consciousness of his circumstances. Through them he
> communicates with the universe.[3]

This circumstance of which Ortega writes is nothing other than
the discovery of the problem of life. That is, early on Ortega realized
that the fundamental point of departure of any genuine philosophy
should be grounded in an attempt to come to terms with vital human
existence. This Marburg period is thus the crucial period in his life
when he begins to view man as a kind of poetic tragic hero who
is trapped on a stage of personal circumstances. It was Hermann
Cohen, whom Ortega called his teacher and who incited Ortega
to think of life as a constant flux of creating and re-creating. It was
also Cohen, according to Ortega, who brought him to conceive of
human life as the fundamental reality. Ortega writes:

> From Cohen I learned to extract the feeling of drama that
> in fact inheres in every great intellectual problem or, better
> still, that every ideological problem is.[4]

Ortega's stay at Marburg influenced him even further in his
desire to critique the inherent dangers of naive realism. Yet his neo-
Kantian schooling also inspired in him a feeling of philosophical
rebellion that led to the negation of absolute idealism that is such a
dominant feature of his mature thought. Ortega went to Marburg
already preoccupied with the task of Europeanizing Spain. What
he attempted to do was equivalent to re-educating the Spanish
populace in all things European. He viewed Spain as a nation whose
time had already come and gone. He saw Spain as an intellectual
novice not fully prepared to understand the technological nuances
of the twentieth century.

Thus, his schooling at Marburg was to serve as a firsthand
preparation for creatively undertaking the task of reformer. What
he left behind in Spain was a pragmatic and to some extent anti-
intellectual tradition frozen in the colonial tracks of the previous

century. What Ortega encountered at Marburg must have come as a shock to him because he felt that he had turned 180 degrees and landed right in the arms of a "forced" doctrine which, according to him, forged truthfulness where none was to be found.[5]

The future Spanish circumstance, as he saw it, would one day parallel Socrates' notion that "man cannot sustain a life where there is no longing for truth." Yet ironically, he quickly began to interpret neo-Kantian philosophy as a banal use of reason where "never before has a lack of truthfulness played such a large and important role in philosophy."[6] Ortega clearly saw neo-Kantian thought to be static and not reasonably equipped to close the immense gulf between the highly detached and theoretical world of science and the immediate and spontaneous dictates of daily life. This theme would eventually penetrate into all of his mature work. Still, what he inadvertently found at Marburg was the necessary impetus to undertake his task of reformer. The Spanish circumstance, viewed as a "vaguely" rational society trapped in a technological age, became for Ortega a central rallying point in his reasoning.

Ortega's experience at Marburg, which he called a "Kantian prison," started out as a search for metaphysical principles on which to ground reflection but ended up in the development of a critical approach to theoretical thought as a whole. Thus, in retrospect, it is safe to interpret Cohen's influence on the mature thought of Ortega as carrying more of a negative impulse than a positive one. What the neo-Kantian tradition at Marburg actually did was to alienate Ortega from a total engagement in speculative metaphysics. Rather than concerning himself with pure reason and logic, he instead directed his attention to a methodical study of the structure of human life. If one keeps in mind that Ortega's greatest concern was the Spanish circumstance at the turn of the century, then it becomes clear why he opted for a more metaphysical approach to philosophical problems as opposed to a merely neo-Kantian metaphysical solution.

The apparent impotence of Neo-Kantian thought in effectively closing the gap between the phenomenal and the noumenal life-world engendered in Ortega the desire to concentrate on the anthropological question, "What is man?" This problem, he thought, must be analyzed from the perspective of history as human vitality, since for him history is the totality of the acts of individual consciousness. Hence, when Ortega left Marburg, his dissatisfaction with neo-Kantian thought allowed him to turn toward the life-world philosophies of thinkers such as Bergson, Croce, Husserl, and later Dilthey. By 1914 his energy was completely directed at what he called "reflection on the phenomenon of human life." His first essay on the structure of human life is to be found in his 1910 publication titled "Adam in Paradise," to which we will now turn.

Part II The Dialectic of Experience: "Adam in Paradise"

Ortega's notion of relations involves seeing circumstances as molding or determining our being, because in his estimation man is the totality of his circumstances. Thus all concreteness is made possible by an endless array of relations. However, relations Ortega argues are never simply a Cartesian "res." Instead, they are always ideas. This is why he views the whole history of modern philosophy as idealism. Adam therefore finds himself looking inward and interiorizing reality, since he is the one correlating the many abstract entities that make up his consciousness. In essence, Ortega's major point in this early essay is to argue that man's initial philosophical discovery is his own consciousness and not the objects of common sense. Thus any degree of wonder concerning the external world must follow this fundamental premise. As a result of this line of reasoning, Ortega draws a very subtle distinction between idealism and realism. He accepts idealism only insofar as it attributes primacy to consciousness, but does not become a precondition for the independence of the self from material objects. Hence for Ortega the external world is never absolute and overbearing even though it nevertheless remains independent of consciousness. The objective world remains at the mercy of consciousness as a subject of interpretation, organization, and generalization.

What Ortega does in "Adam in Paradise" is to "collapse" or reduce realism into idealism, since only ideas can unify and give meaning to the universe. "I am I and my circumstances" is possible because, according to Ortega, the true idealist immerses himself in the material world and thus makes it his concern to make sense of its being. The reality of the world as an independent entity can never be fully grasped because the coming to consciousness of the universe as a totality of relations is an infinite procedure. What is known, in effect, is the world as a limited idea of consciousness. He states:

> The outside world is within us, it exists in our power of formulating ideas. The world is my production, and my image—as the rough Schopenhauer will say roughly. The ideal is the real. Strictly speaking, and in pure truth, only the idea-producing, the thinking, the conscious exists; I, I myself, me Ipsum.[7]

In section 6 of "Adam in Paradise," Ortega offers his answer to the question, "What is man?" Since Adam finds himself totally alone in the world, human life is interpreted as a soliloquy. This monologue in fact showcases the nature of consciousness. The initial stage of Adam's discovery in respect to the structure of life is therefore first and foremost the discovery that human life always appears as differentiated. Human life is always that which is concrete and self-conscious.

Authentic life, according to Ortega, is always striving toward individuality and concreteness. Hence, to live is to create and re-create the totality that is the universe. This is why life is in essence a drama or aesthetic creation that should attempt to re-create the ideal that man carries within him as a heroic or tragic being. Thus human life is always in the process of individualization. Yet this individualization can never take place apart from our individual circumstances that frame and shape our being. Therefore, life is coexistence-with-things as well. The unifying structure of life is to be seen in the individual perspective, which organizes reality rather than deforming it. However, Adam's discovery of himself as consciousness is as great or perhaps a greater concern than his coming to terms with the objective world. He explains:

> I am not a substantial being nor is the world, but we both are in active correlation: I am that which sees the world and the world is that which is seen by me. I exist for the world and world is that which is seen by me. I exist for the world, and the world exists for me.[8]

"Adam in Paradise," we realize, can be characterized as an attempt to classify or identify the being of man against a material and static background. This early essay serves as an ontological study of reality that sets up a hierarchy of "being" whereby the being of man as problematic takes precedence. As an ontological inquiry concerning the question, "What is man," the essay dissects the existence of man as follows. First, a distinction is made between the two forms of life: biological and biographical, where man partakes in the former by way of the latter. Second, biographical life, contrary to mere biological life, is always singular, concrete, and self-conscious. Yet the immediate nature of self-consciousness cannot be continuously maintained, thus creating the necessity for the affirmation of the external world. This mutual dependency brings about Ortega's notion of life as coexistence with things, which was later to become the cornerstone of his philosophy. And finally this dialectic culminates in man's coexistence with the world, which in effect makes man yet another entity of the world, but as man-in-the-world.

From this we realize that the necessary and continual friction that man has with his circumstances keeps man from falling into solipsism. Hence the notion of life as narrative that Ortega employs is not just a colorful metaphor. Life as narrative expresses the essential dynamic character of man to whom "things" constantly happen. Thus life-as-lived friction between individual consciousness and the world becomes the foundation of human reality. External reality then, as opposed to inner reality, can be grasped only due to the self-reflective starting point found in human life. It is from this immediate radical reality that one can branch out onto the rest of reality that subsequently constitutes the totality of the external world.

During this perspectivist period, which lasted from 1910 to 1923, Ortega managed to put some objective distance between his notion of consciousness and naive realism. His refutation of the autonomy and independence of the external world is firmly grounded in his notion of consciousness as preceding matter. What is not yet entirely clear is the argument whereby he refutes idealism as well, which is precisely from where his notion of vitalism begins. An essential question left unanswered in this early period is that: If life is all activity and execution, then from where is it that the impetus to create oneself in one's image arises, since reflection is the essential ingredient necessary for life as an existential project? The impact of this dilemma can be seen in the following passage from *Phenomenology and Art*:

> But since life in its very "substance" is circumstantial, it is obvious that although we may think otherwise, everything we do is done in view of our circumstances. This allows us to discover the true function of the intellect and of culture. Life confronted with circumstances is "uncertainty," "shadows," "a problematic question," "preoccupation," "insecurity."[9]

But what avenue remains open to attempt to comprehend these questions if the essence of life is activity and execution? To this question, Ortega adds:

> By the same token, life needs "clarity," "security," "self-control." Now then, this clarity, this complete control is interpretation—clarification, explanation, or exegesis—of life.[10]

He points to a possible answer by stating that "culture, art, science or politics—is the commentary, that mode of life in which life itself acquires polish and neatness through internal refraction."[11] We must interpret culture; it seems, as any of the possible dynamic modes in which human life can be lived. Moreover, "Adam in Paradise" itself raises the question of whether philosophical thought is natural to man. Or if it is imposed upon him by science, culture, art, or religion. If man's primary activity is to act, then this instinctual mode of being seems to leave very little room for reflection, thus undermining man's ability to solve the enigma of life-as-project. Ortega writes:

> Man's destiny, this is primarily action. We do not live to think, on the contrary: we think in order that we may succeed in surviving.[12]

This line of thought is also readily visible in the first paragraph of his book *What Is Philosophy?* There, Ortega alludes to the notion of not announcing in advance one's direction in thinking since one cannot anticipate the exigencies of the thought process. But here we must question whether the general direction of thought is not already predisposed the moment that the question is brought forth. But, to this assertion he responds:

> But, as we shall see, a thought that is separated from the mental road that leads toward it, a thought standing alone and abrupt as an island, is an abstraction in the worst sense of the word, and by the same token is unintelligible.[13]

Yet in this paragraph, where action is seen to take precedence over thought, Ortega nevertheless emphasizes reflective thought to unveil truth. This undoubtedly creates a fundamental tension in his writing that we will return to in greater detail in the next chapter. He states:

Every intellectual effort sets us apart from the commonplace, and leads us by hidden and difficult paths to secluded
spots where we find ourselves amid unaccustomed thoughts.
These are the results of our meditation.[14]

There is one more aspect of Ortega's early thought that we
should keep in mind as we take up this question regarding the need
for reflection and its relation to action. This has to do with a dualistic
notion of reality as consisting of two levels: a primary (patent) and
a secondary (latent) level. Ortega places reflection on the secondary
level. The first level of reality includes the following: 1) color, 2)
sound, 3) pain and pleasure. When confronting this primary level of
reality, man is passive. The second level of reality includes: 1) science,
2) art, 3) justice, 4) courtesy, 5) religion, and so on. Thus, the first
level is one of sense data and impressions. This level is a naturalistic
one unmistakably evident to any sentient being. On this level man
is engaged in what Ortega calls "passive looking," whereby nothing
other than a chaotic conglomeration of impressions is revealed, but
which does not necessarily constitute the reality of the world. It is on
the second level of reality that man engages in "active seeing." This
level is equivalent to interpretation. The profoundness of the world
as comprehended on this level requires more effort on our part than
is needed for the latent and superficial world of impressions.

This dualistic split in reality acts as the grounding force in
Ortega's philosophy of perspective. By construing reality to consist
of a passive and an active side, where man is responsible for the
latter, reality as man apprehends it becomes perspectival. To say
this in another way, Adam's awakening in Paradise is the result of
a mutual dependency between his consciousness and a material
world that forces him to reflect. Ortega's point is that man originally
discovers himself existing amongst a cornucopia of images that are
meaningless apart from his being conscious of them. He adds:

The need to see created seeing. Thus vision itself created the
seeing instrument. In other words: the function creates the

organ. And what creates the function? Necessity, of course. And what creates necessity? The problem?[15]

Ortega's project in "Adam in Paradise" is therefore an attempt to refute realism without having to embrace idealism wholeheartedly. His desire to surpass the dictates of common sense and particularly naturalism accounts for the friction that is to be found in all of his mature writing. This uneasiness and inquietude, in my estimation, is not entirely resolved until his later works. This is why I find it a fruitful line of inquiry to pose the question of whether Ortega's thought is essentially a brand of subjective idealism or rather better understood as ratio-vitalism, a question to which we must now turn.

Part III Ortega's Thought: Idealism or Ratio-Vitalism?

Having paid attention to some key elements in Ortega's intellectual development, it becomes clear that Ortega's main philosophical preoccupation is the synthesis of the empirical world with the subjective "I" in a manner that gives precedence to neither one. His greatest concern is not to fall prey to the logical demands of either idealism or realism. This position in his estimation is achieved by what he calls ratio-vitalism. Yet we must ask: Can he effectively undertake this task and still retain the "I" of radical reality that is not merely spontaneous, but also reflective?

During Ortega's early perspectivist period (1902–1914), his epistemology can be defined as an attempt to seek the limits of reason. His view concerning vital-reason is in essence an attempt at replacing pure reason with vital reason insofar as the latter runs its course through human life. He was to fully develop this idea in his book *The Modern Theme* (1922), which is based on his 1921–1922 university lectures.

Since Ortega's early thought treats human life as the starting point of philosophy, reality is not seen as absolute, but rather as that which depends on individual perspective given that, as he writes, "every life is a point of view directed upon the universe."[16] By attempting to reconcile idealism and realism, this perspectivist epistemology finds no other fixed point of reference than life-as-lived drama, since neither mind nor the objective world cannot have dominion over life itself. During this early period, Ortega already hints at the possibility that, for him, life and vital reason may in fact be synonymous terms. Given this understanding of his early thought, we can equate his notion of perspective with idealism if what we mean by idealism is, as Oliver W. Holmes has stated:

> The view that ideas possess the key to the interpretation and to the understanding of reality and that the mind and spiritual values are fundamental in the world as a whole.[17]

As such, every individual perspective interprets the objective world from its own circumstance, which cannot be duplicated. But is this not tantamount to saying that reality is manifested differently for every individual? And if this is the case, does not perspective become a brand of relativism? Ortega in fact stresses that this is not the case. Thus perspective, not ideas, becomes the anchor of reality. But in questioning this perspectivist epistemology, one must essentially also question what the constitution of the being of man is. If man-as-radical-reality is not idea or spirit, then what essentially is man? Ortega tells us that man is simply life. Nevertheless, this life is not merely biological life as another instance of vegetative or zoological life. Human life is biographical life. Biographical life turns a conscious glance toward itself, thus detaching itself from the rest of nature. Hence, for Ortega naturalism alone cannot explain the "meaning" of human life. But neither does Ortega care to embrace speculative metaphysics head on.

By attempting to reconcile life and reason without losing the necessary vitality that is essential to both concepts, Ortega is forced to make them co dependent. This idea of life as biographical, which he introduces in *Meditations on Quixote*, and that he fully develops in *Man in Crisis*, will become the cornerstone of Ortega's definition of man.[18]

Therefore, having studied in Marburg, Ortega's thought was inevitably influenced by neo-Kantian idealism. Yet his impulse as a thinker compelled him to view ideas as dependent on human life and never as a theoretical exercise. Thus Ortega refers to man as a "fabricator of universes," out of a vital and critical necessity to survive.[19] This is the very same thing that Camus argues for in his work *The Myth of Sisyphus*. Reason for Ortega is the result of a vital need to make sense of the world of which man is an inheritor:

> Reason, at its most authentic, is vital reason. This means strictly and concretely, that the intellect or pure reason alone, does not create basic concepts but is driven to them by vital necessity.[20]

Therefore, "first live and later philosophize" becomes Ortega's philosophical point of departure through an assertion that we philosophize because we live. This is essentially the argument that he sets forth in "Adam in Paradise" and which underscores in his refutation of idealism. He can be called a metaphysical philosopher in that he seeks answers to the ultimate existential concerns that pertain to man. In Ortega's case, metaphysics takes the form of the "interiority" that man embodies. This notion of interiority is as real, if not more so, as the external world. However, Ortega, like Kant, rejects any absolute idealism that would grant ideas the autonomy of existing prior to the external world. Like Kant, Ortega does not view ideas or pure reason as the ultimate reality. Instead, the true power of reason lies in man's capacity to experience and comprehend the dictates of the material world.

Furthermore, the crucial and deciding factor by which Ortega embraces ratio-vitalism as a mediator between idealism and realism is what must be understood as the "Spanish circumstance." After leaving Marburg, Ortega's true passion became that of reforming Spanish pedagogy and intellectual society. This was a mundane and practical task that would have to take the form of practical reason, not theoretical reason.

Human life, if it is to have any outwardly objective meaning and authenticity, must be seen as the individual lived friction that exists between our circumstances and our consciousness. Life as interiority is a constant "happening" to us. That is, life is something that quite literally, according to Ortega, engulfs us. Hence, the reality that is human life can be understood only from within. This philosophy of ratio-vitalism attempts to explain life from the inside out and as projected toward the world, thus giving primacy to interiority. This emphasis on biographical-life-as-drama, Ortega views as being a condition that is natural only to man.

Part IV Life as Radical Reality

Human existence, when defined as biographical rather than biological, can be argued to begin not at the moment of birth or even at conception, but rather at that fleeting instance when self-consciousness of oneself is first reached. For instance, Ortega argues that a child is not confronted with the cosmos, and as such his existence lacks a central radiating point, namely himself, as object of inward reflection. For all practical matters this state can be called innocence, since the child at this stage of life is not yet self-conscious of his role as an entity in space and time. But what is defined as innocence in the child (for example, a pre-pubescent moral/psychological stage of development) is equally referred to as alienation or disorientation in unreflective adults, since the result is the equivalent "to living outside of oneself." This disorientation is the result of not attaining to the level of reflective self-consciousness that is natural in man.

The key element in attempting to systematize the bulk of Ortega's thought, I will argue, is precisely the positing of the "I as a radiating point of reflection," as the initial and fundamental circumstance (radical reality) from which coherence is brought to the universe. Radical reality must not be taken here to mean the most important, exclusive, or even the only reality. Instead, it must be understood as the immediate and thus primary reality with which man must come to terms during a given time in the course of life. If the cosmos is to exist as an objective reality, then there must be a foundational focus-point from which one can engage vis-à-vis with this cosmic reality.

Next, it is important to understand that for Ortega it is not appropriate to speak of "I" as being simply my body as an instance of my circumstance. The "I" that characterizes my essence is never a spatial substance. Hence, the essence of man is never extended. A sustained and insightful reading of Ortega demonstrates that his overriding concern is with the question, "What is man?" As we shall see, comprehending this answer requires that we see how Ortega can maintain that man is not solely a result of his material circumstance, his body, or even his life as a vital biological principle. Man, for Ortega, is certainly not to be referred to as being his body, even though he is his body to the degree that his body is part of the overall circumstance that he must face daily. Instead, man is said to be: 1) "I," 2) self-consciousness awareness, 3) will. But none of these metaphysical characteristics of man can be spatial qualities, since man is not a spatial being. In other words, for Ortega the human body is the vehicle for the exteriorization of that which is totally internal. Nevertheless, the essence of man fails to be made totally external, since these characteristics are never quantifiable. Therefore this metaphysical definition of human life as internal is in essence indicative of Ortega's definition of life as biographical.

Furthermore, the intimacy that exists between human life and the self-conscious I can be grasped only through the body, which acts as mediator. Intimacy (essence) is never seen by itself, but rather always along with the body as a further instance of circumstance. The function of the body when viewed in metaphysical terms is to manifest outwardly the subjective essence of man in the objective plane. An effective explanatory analogy might be to say that what space is to the body, the body is to the self-conscious I. The point is that the body is what it is as a physical entity, but at the same time it is much more than just the carnal vitality that it alludes to.

The body alludes to that which contains meaning, and in this sense the body is expressive. It is certain that the body as an organic objective reality remains the object of quantification as well as qualification as an object of study. It is also our closest circumstance in relation to ourselves, but it is not the self. This is a dualistic interpretation, but as I have stated earlier, Ortega's thought can be construed as dualistic.

The search for a fundamental reality in Ortega's thought is not initially easily settled given the dualistic structure of his thought. But Ortega's refutation of commonsense realism lies in deemphasizing its stubborn, overbearing, and apparent independence from man. He attempts to attribute less of an independent and autonomous role to biological life than he allots to consciousness as it pertains to biographical life.[21] On the other hand, we have already stated that he is unwilling to embrace idealism wholeheartedly either, mainly due to his refusal to ground all objective reality on consciousness.

The problem lies in that Ortega's last remaining obstacle in order for him to embrace idealism is the problem of solipsism. His sole concern and thus his purpose in attempting to mediate between realism and idealism is his concern that the discovery of the primacy of the self-conscious self will become dominant, thus annihilating the objectivity of external reality. It was solipsism that troubled him most, and therefore the condition of the body as one's most immediate circumstance is used by Ortega to link biographical life with the material world.

Thus to summarize, Ortega argues that only through one's circumstance can one come to reflect upon oneself. This is the fundamental dialectic of the lived experience, one that demonstrates that it takes different situations, circumstances, and experiences for us to discover our "I" of consciousness. What Ortega attempts to avoid by all means is the notion that subjectivity can fashion itself to exist independently of the external world, as is the case in his understanding of Descartes. Ortega will agree that the existence of external objects is never secure without a subject to witness them, but in order to avoid falling back onto the "natural attitude," he develops the notion of the coexistence of the I with its circumstances.[22]

Nevertheless, the problem of fundamental reality persists. If it is argued that all reality radiates from my I as a point of departure as a reflective "I" whereas all other entities are said only to exist, it would seem to follow that I am the fundamental reality. Also, when Ortega speaks of life, it is always only my life that is at issue and never collective biological life. This being the case, he must conclude that all reality is secondary to my own awareness of myself. But how then can it be possible that the discovery of the world can take place prior to the discovery of the self? Ortega's answer to this is that circumstances force man to think in order for him to survive. In his estimation, reflection is a secondary act that enables one to survive in the natural world. Hence, man reflects through coercion and not necessarily at random.

Thus to conclude this chapter, we see that, for Ortega, man-as-radical-reality is in essence the end result of a dialectical process of discovery that makes man aware of his circumstances as a metaphysical problem. The friction that is present between man's will and his circumstances creates the necessity for man to know himself.

Man-as-radical-reality is Ortega's answer to the question, "If neither idealism nor realism, then what?" Man is ontologically the starting point of any reflective and critical philosophy and the keeper of the torch of being, as it were. It seems apparent that if the task is neither to attribute precedence to the external world nor to subjectivity, then a third position that brings about a synthesis of the two must be sought. The result of this dialectical synthesis culminates in man-as-radical-reality as the result of a dialectical oscillation between the subjective I and external reality. But if the reality of man takes precedence due to the fact that man attributes reality to external entities with thought, is this not to fall back into our original point of questioning? To this objection Ortega will reply that no one can doubt the external world. Also, he will make the claim that if the world is purely mental, "then why is it extended and thus detached from me?" This is the very point of contention that keeps Ortega from embracing neo-Kantianism wholeheartedly. To this point he writes:

> The tragedy of idealism stems from the fact that having transmuted the world as an alchemist might, into "subject," into the content of subject it enclosed this subject within itself; then there was no way of explaining clearly how, if this theatre is only my image and a piece of me, it appears to be so completely different from me.[23]

However, regardless of this objection that Ortega makes concerning the primacy of the self, he nevertheless places more weight on the self than on the independence of external entities. While he implicitly and explicitly argues that things can have no reality independent of a subject, it remains the subject that, while not existing encapsulated within itself, nevertheless does give transcendence to the external world. But following this line of inference, Ortega would apparently have to argue that, for example, prior to its discovery on March 13, 1930, by Clyde W. Tombough, the planet Pluto was nonexistent for all practical purposes, and thus any theorizing concerning it would be nonsensical. But to this we must respond that the ninth planet was not a mental creation of Tombough or Percival Lowell prior to him. Pluto, like the other astronomical bodies, for example, dark matter, pulsars, quasars and so on, existed prior to their recent discovery. This being the case, Ortega's understanding of "coexistence with" must be interpreted to mean, more appropriately, "awareness of." Awareness of is more appropriate than "coexistent with" because the former has more of a self-conscious and immediate connotation than the latter, which connotes a spatial relation and gives priority to the objects we exist with.

Hence, I will contend that man-as-radical-reality falls ontologically under the aegis of idealism if what is meant by idealism is the view that mind and spirit are fundamental in the universe as a whole, without having to negate external entities.[24] We will further develop this thought by showing how it is that man can "orient" himself only through the process of *ensimismamiento* by reflecting and thus "removing" himself as much as possible from the material world. Therefore, I must conclude this chapter by asserting that Ortega's thought is always metaphysical in nature due to his inexhaustible concern with the structure of human life from within. This very central notion of interiority will be taken up in the following section.

Chapter Two

Ortega y Gasset's introduction to neo-Kantianism while studying at the University of Marburg from 1906 to 1908 was to serve the young, twenty-three-year-old Spaniard as a philosophical epiphany.[1] Studying with Herman Cohen and Paul Natorp taught Ortega to view self-conscious human existence as the ultimate and irreducible form of life. Also while at Marburg, Ortega learned to critique what he called the commonsense reasoning of naive realism. But equally, too, he began a lifelong attempt to refute the absolute idealism so prevalent at Marburg. From this encounter with neo-Kantianism, the major themes found in Ortega's work are 1) life as a poetic-existential undertaking, 2) human life as biographical existence, 3) vital reason as the immidiate, differentiated ground of historical reason, 4) human existence as drama or narrative, 5) life as *que-hacer* (having-to-do, project), and 6) life as radical reality emerged. Thus, what I shall argue in this essay is that this intellectual awakening of Ortega's after returning to Spain becomes already quite clear in his first publication, "Adam in Paradise," a work that he wrote in 1910. This work serves as an early indication of the existential and phenomenological direction that his work was to take. He would fully develop these themes in his first book, *Meditations on Quixote*, a work published four years later. However, his earliest concerns are with the exploration of human life as that, which due to its self-conscious nature, surpasses all renditions of man as merely biological. These central themes in Ortega's work are all already present in "Adam in Paradise." Thus in these pages I shall develop the theme of what Ortega refers to as biographical life.

Biographical existence is a self-recognition of our subjectivity, and this becomes manifest as interiority. This, Ortega has proposed, is the distinguishing act of our coming to terms with our individual essence. These developments are equally important in light of existential questions that will be posed by subsequent thinkers such as Heidegger, Sartre, Marcel, and Jaspers, for instance. I have divided this chapter into three parts. In part I, "The Discovery of Interiority," I emphasize Ortega's treatment of Adam's discovery of subjectivity as a sort of anthro-existential "first man." In part II, "The Objective World as My Circumstance," further attention is paid to this subjective inward turn, except that now the emphasis is on the external world as part of my existential circumstance. Part III, "'Yo Soy Yo y Mis Circumstancias' (I Am I and My Circumstances)," works as a rounding-off of Ortega's concern that while realism must be surpassed, subjectivity as well cannot become encapsulated in itself.

Ortega's philosophical task in "Adam in Paradise" is essentially an attempt to surpass the idealist thesis but at the same time not to accept realism wholeheartedly. The significance of this project as far as Ortega scholarship is concerned is the realization that this particular concern, which is dominant throughout the entirety of his philosophical works, is first elaborated in "Adam in Paradise," a very early essay.[2] It is in this work and not in *Meditations on Quixote*, written in 1914, where the aforementioned thesis is first espoused. The foundation of this argument, then, is Ortega's notion of the coexistence between man, a biographical-existential entity, and his external circumstances as a broadening of man's perspective. "Adam in Paradise" is Ortega's discovery of human life as philosophical concern. It is from this work that his idea of life as radical reality evolves. In this work the persona of Adam, even though not necessarily that of the biblical entity, serves the role of a dual metaphor. In its first function, Adam can be seen as representing the discovery of what Ortega calls "the primordial reality of the conscious, of subjectivity."[3] In essence, Adam is the quintessential thinker who doubts and who by doing so removes himself from Paradise. However, this understanding of Paradise, Ortega argues, is equivalent to a view of the prereflective reality of the external world as perceived by the dominant naive realism prior to the pre-Socratics. Realism, thus, according to Ortega, is not only naive and innocent, but always also a primary condition of human consciousness. Yet the second function of Adam as metaphor is to serve as a universal internal principle of self-reflection, which discovers itself having to make sense of the external world. "Adam in Paradise" is in fact the discovery of human life as the biographical and thus subjective pole of human life, and not merely biological life. Ortega explains:

> When Idealism left the reality of the outside world hanging in suspense and discovered the primordial reality of the conscious, of subjectivity, it lifted philosophy to a new level from which the latter cannot slip back under pain of retrogression in the worst sense of the word.[4]

Furthermore, it is important to realize that this biographical notion of human life according Ortega is firmly rooted in man's innate, even though dormant, ability to question his own existence. Wonder and awe remove the would-be thinker from the flat, one dimensionality of the external world of realism. By sidestepping the instinctual, having to pay allegiance solely to his biological circumstances, that is, his body, Adam simultaneously begins to lose his innocence. About this rejection of realism Ortega has the following to say:

> Ancient realism, which starts from the undoubted existence of cosmic things, is philosophic ingenuousness, the innocence of paradise. All innocence is Paradisiacal. Because the innocence of he who neither doubts, distrusts, or suspects, finds himself in the position of ancient and primitive man surrounded by nature, a cosmic landscape, a garden—and this is Paradise.[5]

Part I The Discovery of Interiority

At the very core of Ortega y Gasset's concept of interiority, one initially encounters a perplexing paradox. On one hand, in the

Meditations on Quixote, the reader is to understand the intimacy and immediacy that is biographical human existence as belonging solely to a phenomenon of consciousness, one that is purely inwardly driven or internal in scope. Thus, because of this Ortega argues that the essence of man can never be grasped through the senses, given that man's true being, that is, his metaphysical orientation, is never a spatial phenomenon but rather an inwardly vital one.[6] In the prologue to *Meditations on Quixote,* which he refers to as the preliminary meditation, there appears a warning to the perspective reader about the nature of the questions that Ortega will engage in this work. Among these questions he includes the metaphysical importance of silence, both literal as well as metaphorical. Silence, he tells us, is always a required prerequisite to self-knowledge. Thus silence, when viewed as the result of a monologue with oneself, sets the stage for self-contemplation, much the same as interaction with the world allows us to know our physical circumstances. Silence in this instance must be interpreted to mean contemplation. However, on the other hand, regardless of the importance attributed to silence in Ortega's estimation, silence can never be absolute given that his overall philosophical project refutes any notion of absolutes. But also, we must add that while it remains true that silence enables one to know oneself, this self-conscious awareness can never occur in a vacuum, but rather within the arena of one's circumstances. This being the case, silence, Ortega argues, cannot be interpreted as solely the droning background effect of "nothingness."

Ortega emphasizes man's coexistence with his circumstances in *Meditations on Quixote* while simultaneously maintaining the view in the preliminary meditation that one's body is also part of our circumstance. *Meditations on Quixote* is a work that attempts to come to terms with the ancient problem of appearance and reality. This was to be a three-part work, however, volumes 2 and 3 never materialized. This work has baffled many critics into thinking that Ortega was merely attempting to write literary criticism. This is not the case. *Meditations* is a multilayered work that offers Ortega's existential-phenomenological rendition of reality. Ortega begins the book with a lucid and literary description of the forest that surrounds El Escorial [7] in which the writer finds himself. But the totality of these woods is never encountered as a forest. Instead, it first appears to him as an otherwise incoherent conglomeration of towering oaks and ashes. Here the trees create a blanket over the sky, which keeps out all but the most indirect and stubborn slivers of sunlight. As can well be expected, the silence that engulfs one in such a desolate place is perennial, and any wayward visitor quickly finds himself as an alien in his own company. But this is precisely, Ortega argues, the authentic and thus confrontational character of solitude, which enables us to listen to our own pulsating heart. When finding ourselves in such circumstances—Ortega calls it threatening—there is, then, no other recourse but to face this silence and embrace our immediate consciousness of ourselves as an exaltation of our existence. Therefore, silence can never be absolute given that one can never be totally alone. There always remains the "murmur of the heart, the subtle action of breathing and the throbbing of the blood in our temples."[8] The parallels to be drawn between this notion of life as interiority and the connection that this engenders to one's physical circumstances warrants some degree of inquiry given that both are equally important as circumstances.

Our first point of questioning concerning Ortega's idea of interiority should be to understand that Ortega's thought, much like that of Descartes, is wholly and intricately dualistic, even though not necessarily by intent. His main concern as a ratio-vitalist thinker is to expose the limits of pure reason and exalt the practical function of vital reason as the latter becomes manifest in human existence. But given Ortega's thought on objective reality as emanating from self-consciousness, which is fundamental to any understanding of reality, one undoubtedly arrives at the conclusion that contemplation concerning the primacy of the self must logically take due precedence in his work. Hence the philosophy of Ortega can be characterized as a study of the self as the foundational denominator of reality.

In section 6 of "Adam in Paradise" he espouses the view that human life is always and foremost a struggle toward individualization. Life is always unique, concrete, and personal, and never collective or abstract. From the outset of his awakening to a state of self-consciousness of himself, what Adam discovers is not simply biological life as representative of the complexities of a living organism situated in space and time. Instead, what Adam discovers is life as problem, that is, biographical life, or life as existential inward possibility. Because of this discovery, life becomes a contemplative question. At this point, life becomes a having-to-do with the surrounding world, which up to now was not detached from my life. Reality for Adam during this early stage of discovery is indeed solely rooted in his self-consciousness of his life as a separate entity from the world. Ortega writes:

> The reality of life consists, then, not in what it is for him who sees it from without, but in what it is for him who is it from within, for him who is living it and in the measure that he lives it.[9]

This existential discovery that Adam makes is not of the theoretical kind such as a formula or theorem that is purely speculative in intent. Instead, this existential encounter fundamentally amounts to the discovery of himself as an object of his reflection. This inward glance we call subjectivity. If taken literally, this initial discovery of the self of the "first man" would most probably only interest anthropologists, sociologists, and theologians. But when taken as a metaphor for the discovery of self-consciousness, we see that Ortega's interest lies in the uncovering of the necessary conditions for the development of self-contemplation.

The reason that Adam can postulate his life as a fundamental and coherent reality is because of his immediate association with the world in which he finds himself. Thus metaphysics, according to Ortega, can never be a purely intellectual and superfluous activity that man utilizes to pass the time. Metaphysics is never a luxury but a vital human necessity. Metaphysics is instead the "lived" and central aspect of human life by which man becomes acquainted with his being.[10] In Ortega's estimation, self-conscious thought develops only after the material circumstances become a problem for us and thus necessitate reflection. Metaphysics, when viewed in this Ortegan context, therefore can only mean the act of situating and categorizing of human existence among an entire spectrum of entities. But this conscious entity recognizes itself at once to be like no other. Self-consciousness perhaps, according to Ortega, becomes the matrix of human perspectival reality. This can be compared to salvation in a religious context, except that the problems of metaphysics emanate as an existential vital force to be reckoned with from within: "Metaphysics is not a science; it is the construction of the world, and that, constructing a world out of circumstances, is human life."[11]

Individual human life, then, can be only what it is because it is circumstantial. To be circumstantial is to delineate the immediate and inwardly directed from the external and objectifying. That is, our life is what it is because we are a totality of all the things that we do and all that surrounds us. This is why in section 11 of "Adam in Paradise," Ortega implicitly argues that realism must be referred to as idealism because ideas unify and give meaning to the universe. But idealism for Ortega takes on a new meaning, one that is central to human contemplation. Hence from this, we are to understand that the true idealist is one who immerses himself in the material world in order to attempt to successfully make sense of his being.

"Adam in Paradise," when viewed as a metaphor and not merely as biblical exegesis, is Ortega's launching pad, as it were, for concentrating on the problem of human existence. As such, "Adam in Paradise" can be translated to mean "Adam in a Prereflective State of Consciousness." This state of paradise is none other than man's initial state of being, where man is not quite self-conscious of himself as a being situated in a world of objects. Adam as a preself-conscious entity is therefore a prereflective being.

Adam's awakening to himself raises the question of whether

indeed, "all men by nature have a desire to know," as Aristotle states at the beginning of Book I of his *Metaphysics,* or is man coerced to "know" by his circumstances in order to survive? This also brings up the related question of whether Adam reflects on his own existence due to an innate existential condition. If the former is true, another appropriate question then becomes, "What must these conditions be?" However, if it is the case that a reflective interiorizing mode exists as an operative innate condition of man, then certainly man is bound or determined to turn inward regardless of his given particular circumstances. If it is the case instead that man reflects upon himself due to coercion from external conditions, then reflective thought is not a unique endowment of nature but rather a tool utilized by man in order to survive. These external conditions may dictate the concrete form that reflection takes. These are all reasonable questions in terms of Ortega's philosophical project.

It is within the structure of these material circumstances that Ortega grounds his ontology. For Ortega, the notion of thinking in a vacuum (situationless) is an absurdity. Reflective thought must always have a provocation. Hence Adam's existential awakening comes about through what he calls a "mediate necessity." That is, a necessity or impetus to reflect that is born outside of oneself. In one way this mediate necessity directs conscious thought away from itself as its own object of reflection. But also, through this engagement with external entities can total absorption in self-reflection develop. In fact, the necessary condition that creates the zest or desire for knowledge cannot in and of itself bring about knowledge prior to the outward manifestation of some desired entity. The consequences of this view come to full fruition when Ortega explains that the only manner in which man can contemplate his own existence is by oscillating his reflection between the reality that constitutes the material world and that, which is opposed to it, the self. This is the sequence of reflection that brings about the realization of man's coexistence with the world as reality. This inherent tension in man's life establishes itself as just one more example of a circumstance. This vital fluctuation constitutes the dialectic of the lived experience and thus the authenticity required of biographical life. He explains:

> Apart, I repeat, from the fact that it is not desire which leads to knowledge, but necessity. The desire does not exist unless the thing desired existed earlier, in reality or at least in imagination. That which does not even exist at all cannot provoke desire.[12]

If Adam is to awaken at all, it follows that this "awakening" must follow a previous state of existential dormancy. But this notion not only engenders a problematic unsteadiness concerning consciousness; it also gives birth to a dialectical paradox.[13]

This paradox is one having to do with the inherent differences between what Ortega has called the biographical versus the biological constitution of man. There is no doubt that Adam has existed as a sentient being prior to his coming to terms with his own existence. Nevertheless, it can be argued that Adam's dormant state of existence has in fact resembled the biological and thus vegetative existence of plant and animal life. This aspect of our questioning does logically entail that Adam cannot effectively engage in philosophical reflection while in this prereflective posture of being. At issue here is the question of the psychic states at work preceding the realization of self-conscious reflection. This being the case, one must ask, "What constitutes the life of prereflective Adam?" Prereflective Adam does not merely coexist with things, since in order to coexist, according to Ortega, he would have to be aware of his spatial-existential position among them. Neither can he view his life as a problem, since in order to do so he must orient himself reflectively. In other words, if Adam is to orient himself existentially, he must first attain a perspective on the world that surpasses that the senses engender. The role of perspective, then, is to unify and organize reality into a coherent structure.

Perspective allows for differentiation through individualization. In this regard, Ortega's thought can be said to resemble Schopenhauer's, for instance, since the dynamic nature of interior dialectic is constantly forcing man toward a separation from the generic.[14] Perspective enables man to develop spatial-temporal awareness through the process of individualization. Space, then, is the material vehicle through which the "I" of consciousness can coexist with external entities. Individual perspective is what enables Ortega to view metaphysics, therefore, as a uniquely human endeavor that attempts to coalesce all human experiences. The method of metaphysics, then, like that of art, for Ortega, is always one that calls for concreteness and individualization.

Perspective is born out of necessity. Furthermore, perspective is born out of a vital reason that is coerced into existence by a vital necessity called life. Adam's dormancy comes to an end as a biological entity when the vital necessity of self-conscious thought realizes itself. Hence, Adam's being-outside-himself, as it were, in his inauthentic prereflective stage of being is a necessary prologue to the vitality that the biological being can ascend to.

In a manner of speaking, Adam's existential orientation is truly a reorientation, since what he is doing is tantamount to a discovering and not an inventing of subjectivity. Rather than positing the "I" of consciousness within the preexisting structure of material reality, Adam instead finds the "I" of consciousness within himself.

The discovery of interiority is the discovery of the primacy of the self vis-à-vis a superimposed structure (universe) that lies outside of this newly found human reality that now becomes manifest as the self. While it is true that a realist theory of human reality places man at the center of the universe, as is the case, for instance, with Renaissance humanism, it remains equally true that existential human reality is the starting point of all philosophical endeavor, since individual human life as an existentially self-conscious entity is the measure of all logos and coherence. To this end Ortega writes: "Metaphysics is sought by man in order to find out his basic orientation."[15]

The fundamental difference between self-conscious and

prereflective Adam is found in what Ortega calls *reparar*, which is that which traditionally has been called "being self-conscious of something," and *contar con*, which means to rely on, or to be aware of. The gulf between these two definitions is considerable and worth pointing out, since they are fundamental to our understanding the difference between mechanical biological living as *contar con* and self-conscious existence or *reparar*. *Contar con* can essentially be characterized as equivalent to walking up a flight of stairs, which one at that moment totally takes for granted. *Reparar*, on the other hand, is the inward necessity to wonder that begets philosophical questioning. *Reparar* is equivalent to asking oneself the meaning and worth of one's life; for instance, when confronted with a fatal disease. As fundamental as these two states of mind are to human life, they are not realized or exercised until one is faced with one's external circumstances.[16] To this point we will now turn.

Part II The Objective World as My Circumstance

In this section I will concentrate solely on the physical aspect of circumstance, that is, the external world. Since it is the case that circumstance does not just denote the physical conditions of one's life but also economic, political, and cultural factors as well as convictions, beliefs, intuition, and the like, a distinction must be made concerning the diverse manifestations of circumstance.

We may begin by stating that at the outset of all life there are crude and self-evident appearances that do not challenge or surpass the appeal of common sense. The world as a vital clump of organic matter orbiting a distant sun 93 million miles away is the essential, thus the foremost circumstance common to all mankind. This fact allows for the basic universal situation of man. Hence man's physical anchorage as circumstance is and has always been planet earth.

Pointing out the two fundamentally different aspects of circumstance—that it is always material and that it always involves life—

will enable us to later understand Ortega's notion of authenticity. In the first place, the outward reality that is the external world is an essentially passive primary reality appealing to the senses. This is the patent world, or as Ortega refers to it, the *mundo patente,* that is constituted solely by impressions. Our material circumstances as passive entities in themselves thus reveal very little about human reality. However, this patent reality is unmistakably evident to any sentient being. This "lazy" reality involves us only to the degree that hearing, touching, and seeing are concerned. But this passive "looking" reveals nothing other than a chaotic conglomeration of impressions and thus not a coherent world. The material circumstance at this level never engages the intellect, strictly speaking. That is, there arise no questions concerning the immediacy of the world in regard to human life, since the world is merely something external to one and does not yet constitute an existential-pole-as-problem of contemplation for us. Hence the question arises as to how it is possible for a "passive" reality, such as the external world, to provoke one to reflection? Our task now becomes one of inquiring into how it can be possible to close the gulf between this patent reality and the self-reflection that it brings about, if we are to grant that reflection is born out of necessity.

According to Ortega, the reality and profoundness of the world as a problem of philosophical inquiry is slow to manifest itself and thus cannot reveal any substantial truth at the patent level. In fact, it is only after this initial stage has been surpassed that this profound reality becomes evident. This impressionistic world that first appears to the senses is essentially a world of appearance, a nonengaging conglomeration of brute reality pertaining solely to apparent matters-of-fact. This latent world is merely a "superficial" world without any depth. However, already man's initial material circumstance, biological life, places him outside of himself. This world of impressions is also a world of light, color, sound, pain, and pleasure. So that this first level of circumstance becomes the prereflective world of naive-realism. But, since it is the case that Ortega's philosophy never attempts to completely deny material reality but rather always exalts the value and purpose of vital-reason, the epistemological split in the nature of these two levels is never accounted for and therefore exists rather ambiguously throughout his work.

The other fundamental aspect of circumstance is that it is the backdrop, the stage, of our biographical life, our life being our primary circumstance, our radical reality. But life at this level is never merely identical to the self-conscious I. Life as well as the material circumstance exists prior to one's reflecting upon it. The discovery of life is a dual discovery always consisting of finding life within the structure of the material circumstance, in and of itself. Expressed in Cartesian language, we can say that human life always involves a *res-extensa* and a *res-cogitans*. Human reality is a constant fluctuation and strain between these two. If we are to understand how "I am I and my circumstances," the understanding of this vital strain is essential.

Ortega's starting point is his contention that human life is always to be found amongst its circumstances. Circumstance, in return, even when it is merely spoken of as pertaining to objects, is always situational. Thus the "I" which one is, is static, but one's life, viewed as circumstance, is always situational and in constant flux:

> On finding himself alive, man finds himself in a circumstance, a set of surroundings, a world. In this case, the circumstance is this room. My now is my being in a room.[17]

Owing to this situational immediacy, the "now," Ortega can define life as "that something, which happens to us." Hence the structure of "I am I and my circumstance" is at first misleading. If the objective world is the initial circumstance, as the background of existence (not just merely life), this formula must be understood as follows: "I am something, which is not identical to my life, since life is also part of my circumstance." Thus, I am something! Whatever this something may turn out to be, it ("I") must come to terms with my life as circumstance. Thus I am an existential entity that is manifested in something called my life as a vital reality. Therefore, "I am I" is truly "I am," that is, I exist within my life, which turns out to be an event, yet another circumstance.[18] Hence, the entire formula is transformed into, "I am a self-conscious entity manifesting its existence within a vital reality (life) that is spatially and temporally extended in a greater reality, the physical world." To this problematic thought we will now turn our attention in greater detail.

Part III *"Yo Soy Yo y Mis Circumstancias"* (I Am I and My Circumstances)

In this last segment of my essay, we now turn to the understanding of the totality of "my circumstances." My external circumstances, which are essentially a landscape or surrounding, are necessary in framing the possibilities that are my life. However, as essential to my self-awareness of myself as the external circumstances are, the circumstance is in Ortega's estimation a pantomime of the internal man. Moreover, one always discovers the reality of the world prior to discovering oneself. That is, our outer circumstances are only a semblance of inner reality, but it is always known prior to this inner reality. The inference here points to the notion that self-reflection can never occur prior to the discovery of the world-as-fact. But how then can the circumstance be a pantomime of the essence of man, if circumstance is equally applicable to the exteriority that is the body as circumstance?

This problem, I believe, occurs in Ortega's thinking due to the fact that while he wants to break free of the neo-Kantian influence that he was exposed to as a student at Marburg, he nevertheless, as we have previously mentioned, does not want to embrace naive realism. Ortega's reluctance to join the idealist camp wholeheartedly, as well springs from his refusal to posit self-conscious reflection as absolute or to accept the inactivity that he associates with idealism as a viable possibility for man-in-the-world. Since it is the case that

Ortega's thought is essentially a social philosophy, somewhat to the same degree as that of Scheler's and Dilthey's, two of his early influences, he finds it imperative to keep the possibility for man's communicability with the world, especially the social world, open.

It must also be emphasized that Ortega found the generation of '98, which preceded his generation of Spanish intellectuals, to be ineffective and ill suited to the needs of Spanish thought in twentieth-century Europe. Ortega's aim as an intellectual leader of Spain was to Europeanize Spanish thought and thus, as he saw it, to bring the nation up to date with the rest of modern Europe. To this end he writes:

> Nothing is so important for us today, in my opinion, as to sharpen our sensitivity to the problem of Spanish culture, that is, to feel Spain as a contradiction.[19]

This is primarily why Ortega's early essays appeared in the form of newspaper articles in Spain and Buenos Aires. His aim was to feed the Spanish people philosophy in small bits and pieces, and the newspaper offered itself as a viable vehicle for that task. Nevertheless, the consequences of using the newspaper to "educate," as Ortega himself thought possible, also forced him to present his philosophy in what appears to be a limited metaphysical manner. The prevailing philosophy in philosophical circles as well as in the language of the common reader in Spain at that time was pragmatism. The task was to free the common reader from the "security" of his commonsense realism. That is, Ortega understood that to feed German idealism to the common reader was indeed to undermine his own task as educator. His dilemma was therefore to find a mediator between the idealism that he understood to be natural, intuitive, and a reflective impulse and the philosophy of action that he subsequently attempted to develop.

It was toward this end that he founded *España* in 1915, *El Espectador* in 1916, and *Revista de Occidente* in 1923. These publications were very successful, but the end result was that they mostly ended up being read by those in philosophical circles. Nevertheless, it was his hope that some of the ideas contained in these publications would eventually filter down to the benefit of a general populace. It is clear that Ortega's hope in founding these magazines was to attain a higher degree of critical and contemplative environment, where the essence of things was to be placed under a speculative microscope. To this end, he reasons:

> A long experience in teaching and newspaper publishing has forged a rather unfavorable opinion concerning the philosophical capacity of our people in these modern times. Philosophy can only exist breathing an air called mental rigor, precision, and theory.[20]

This notion of educating the general public in philosophical contemplation is not without many profound difficulties. The primary difficulty in bringing about the success of this task lies in the very structure of reflection itself, since, as Ortega had previously said in *Some Lessons in Metaphysics,* metaphysics can exist only for those who need it. By "need it" is meant those who question the status quo of their circumstances. To think metaphysically, in other words, is to dissect and decipher the reality of the world. This option is not open to everyone, as is evident in Ortega's definition of metaphysics: "as being relevant to individual temperament."

However, let us return to the main line of our exposition, which is the basic framework of Ortega's presentation of the discovery of interiority. We see that even though all the connections are not clearly spelled out in detail, perhaps due to the popular format that Ortega uses in order to reach a wider audience, nevertheless for him external circumstances literally serve as the world of our lives, since we are not our life. My life as a vital phenomenon is part of my inner circumstance, but human reality in its fullest form is always equivalent to the situation in which I find myself. Reality is always immediate and my life is always a combination of my subjective "I" plus the external situation in which I find myself at that precise moment in space and time. Human life so understood as situation or circumstance is never static, but rather dynamic. This is why reality is always the now or immediacy. Reality as situational is always manifested as an uncertain present that is projected toward the future, which is equally uncertain.[21]

We have seen Ortega argue that man is not a philosophical entity by nature, but rather that he is coerced into self-conscious reflection by the universe in order to seek order in it. Someone might object, "But isn't the impetus to question natural to man?" To this Ortega will answer that only those who want to surpass the appearances of the external world can become self-conscious of themselves. Only in questioning the circumstances as problematic does man truly orient himself. Circumstances, in Ortega's estimation, allow us to situate ourselves existentially among things. Moreover, given that man can never come to know himself self-consciously in a vacuum, our awareness of our immediacy to ourselves must always be provoked. Man needs some resistance that frustrates his will in order to come to reflect upon himself historically. This is the friction necessary that allows reflection to occur. This view is the core of Ortega's belief that to understand history, we must do so as if it were a narrative that cannot exist without some protagonist. History, then, is foremost a manifestation of historical reason. Viewed as such, history is no other than the external rendition of all the intertwined lives that went to make it.[22]

My circumstances, when constituted of the external world plus my biological life, then, are a prereflective reality that can only become immediate only when vis-à-vis the interior, intimate "I" that is the true essence of man. To exist is always to exist among other things that create a situation for us to live in, but to interpret reality is to find oneself caught in a material web that essentially leads us into finding ourselves as interiority: "On finding himself alive, man finds himself in a circumstance, a set of surroundings, a world.

Therefore, to say "I am I and my circumstances" is not simply to say that one is limited by one's circumstances, as it may first appear. To say "I am I and my circumstances" is a definition of man that can be interpreted as "man is self-conscious of himself only insofar as he is reflective concerning his surroundings." Thus, "know thyself" can never happen immediately, but rather requires a dialectical detour that takes place due to the original fact that man finds himself existing outside himself in the world in the first place. This vital dialectical process of self-orientation culminates in understanding myself as radical reality.[23]

Chapter Three

Part I *Ideas y Creencias* (Ideas and Beliefs)

Ortega's critique of pure reason is founded on the fundamental dualism that constitutes the difference between his notions of ideas and beliefs. Essentially this difference between ideas and the more personal nature of beliefs is equivalent to the difference that he attributes to pure (theoretical) reason and vital-reason. To put it another way, the foundation for vital-reason in Ortega's work is found in the dialectical nature of beliefs that are the core of his thought. By understanding his conception of beliefs, we can begin to grasp his understanding of authenticity and vital-reason as well as his overall philosophical metaphysical anthropology.

When Ortega speaks of beliefs, he is simultaneously laying the foundation for his notion of man as a manifestation of vital-reason. Furthermore, we must keep in mind that what he means by ideas is equivalent with calculative or theoretical reason, and therefore is not what is meant by the vital function of generic ideas. Initially, then, we must define beliefs as: not being ideas at all. Beliefs, as Ortega has said, are not even well-reasoned ideas. Beliefs are not ideas that we possess as we do the shoes that we wear. Instead, the nature of beliefs is rather such that we embody them. Ideas, on the other hand, we can define as: coming from our intellect. Ideas are not vital and as such they are of a secondary nature to living.

It is my belief that Ortega's short essay titled *"Ideas y Creencias"* ("Ideas and Beliefs") can serve as a crucial work for an overall understanding of his thought because there we can see how his notion of dialectic transforms thought per se into the dynamic and vital enterprise that thought must be if it is to be employed in the service of life. For example, when Ortega writes in this essay that metaphysics is an invention of people who need it, he is asserting the primacy of beliefs over pure reason. This is why in presenting his metaphysics of vital-reason as the foundation and immediacy that is biographical life, he maintains that, "While firm in his beliefs, man does not make use of his intellect."[1]

For Ortega, beliefs, in a very strong sense, make up our being or the mode-of-being that we inwardly are as individuals. We can even say that, strictly speaking, we are our beliefs. However, beliefs as modes-of-being are unreflective in that they are not of a calculative nature and therefore we can only exercise our authenticity through the immediacy that our beliefs offer us. That is, we are to others what we truly are to ourselves prereflectively through our beliefs. We manifest our spontaneous self to ourselves as well as to others through a vital immediacy that is necessarily prior to pure reason.

This concept of belief is an implicit semblance of being in the Eleatic sense of the word for Ortega. This is the case even though he does not develop this implication in his work, since he also asserts that man has no nature. However, he does write: "Beliefs are confused with reality itself. They are our world and our being."[2]

We must interpret "our world," in this regard to mean our inner circumstances as being the primal freedoms and limitations that ultimately frame and define us as individuals. Our beliefs sustain our lives, since it certainly is not the case according to Ortega that we can depend on ideas for our moral-existential salvation. Ideas for Ortega are a sort of cognitive "game" that we do not take seriously when it comes to matters of life and death. This critique of pure reason, which he develops during his post-Marburg days, is specifically a reaction to the neo-Kantian "prison" that he experienced while studying there. What Ortega found in Marburg was according to him not philosophy proper, but rather simply an attempt to understand Kant's terminology. To his way of thinking reality itself was never studied at Marburg but rather a positivistic manner of studying pure reason. This is why in 1950, five years prior to his death, he reaffirmed his belief in an essay titled "Medio Siglo de Filosofía" that historical or narrative reason as opposed to pure reason allows for a proper understanding of all things human.[3]

The fundamental point that separates beliefs from ideas is the notion that we count on/with our beliefs as opposed to ideas, which we only think about. Even when not thinking about our beliefs, it is fair to say that we take them for granted, that they aid us in living our life. This essential gulf that divides beliefs and ideas thus has to do with the nature of two distinct modes of being: 1) thinking about something and, 2) Counting on something. What affects our lives without our realizing it must be understood through this form of counting-on. This mode of being is the cog that drives human life, not theory or intellectualizing. It is this immediate prereflective action-reaction manner of living daily life that is the impetus for history, Ortega would argue. Beliefs thus make up the startingpoint or singularity of life. He writes: "Beliefs makeup the base of our lives."[4]

Our beliefs are always the very first point of impact with external reality. They confront us with reality in such a manner that they always remain latent and vital. Once a belief becomes firmly rooted in our temperament, we simply take it for granted, as it aids us in living. At that moment, we begin to count on our beliefs. Our authentic beliefs, for Ortega, are simply the manner in which we choose to exercise our freedom to live. Beliefs also have an ethical dimension to them that is undeniable, since our conduct and manner of using our intellect ultimately depend on our authentic beliefs. This is why Ortega can be said to agree with Ficte's notion that every philosopher will create a system of philosophy according to his own temperament. But this point we will take up in detail in section 4 of this chapter.

At this point, we see however that all of intellectual life is simply the outward polish that is secondary to the authentic self, according to Ortega. What is more, if we can agree with Ortega that all human life naturally seeks individualization and concreteness, then we can understand why he argues that our vehicle for understanding such a vital mechanism is found in our beliefs.[5] Authentic beliefs are merely an immediate manifestation of the self. Therefore, the role of beliefs is to act as the base for human existence. They are the primary source of our coming to know the world, since they are rather spontaneous and not precalculated.

Beliefs are the "basement" of human life, as Ortega calls them, because they are purely passive or receptive in nature. They are passive notions that we possess without the slightest degree of critical activity on our part being necessary for our accepting them. They are the basis of our daily existence.[6]

This is why we can thus describe the basic character of beliefs as being: capricious, habitual, impulsive, and, of course, prereflectively vital in nature. By understanding that Ortega holds beliefs to be ingrained in our being who we are, we come to understand why he relegates thought to a secondary activity of man. For Ortega, as is also the case for Nietzsche as well, the greatest reality to be known is that which pertains to oneself. Nevertheless, if we are "inseparably joined with our beliefs," then in effect we are our beliefs, which consequently would appear to entail that we are pure passivity and that therefore we are molded by the external world (circumstance).[7]

In other words, the problem evident at the heart of Ortega's notion of beliefs is that if he concedes that man is mere passivity, how then can man make his own life as, in effect, Ortega claims he does? If he explains the nature of man as consisting of absolute passivity, then this brand of biologism detracts from man's ability to exist as biographical life. Moreover, if man is solely his beliefs, and these are created or brought about by the essential friction that we maintain with our circumstances, then we could never claim to be "I am I plus my circumstances." In such a case we would simply be our circumstances, and all notions of a personal "I" would perish. This being the case, man would lose the essential freedom that Ortega attributes to man. Man is essentially said to be free because he is first of all placed in a circumstance that he must come to understand as life itself. But also, after man's initial coming to terms with his life as circumstance, he must then adjust this with the external world, which is the circumstance-at-large, as it were.

The fundamental vitality of beliefs is that they are purely to be "counted-on." This notion of having to count on our beliefs, of course, is always immediate in nature in the sense that they are not consciously made into an object of thought or reflection. Nevertheless, because beliefs, according to Ortega, are immediate and vital, they can also be said to be paradoxical. The paradox stems from the fact that while Ortega primarily values beliefs as being vital and as grounding the essence of man, he nevertheless also argues for an existential posture where man must make his own life as project, given that life is never given complete. But in order to undertake such a task, it is necessary that man view life as an existential problem, since this understanding of life as a pressing dilemma to be solved catapults man into action.

Thus, owing to the fluctuation that exists between his dual notions of ideas and beliefs, we must emphasize that man for Ortega is essentially a manifestation of a dialectical metaphysics. This gulf that exists between ideas and beliefs seems to undermine his synthesis of "I am I" with "my circumstances" because it weakens man's ability to make himself in his own image, given that in order to successfully undertake such a task, reflection will be needed.

However, let us return to our exposition of the coexistence of "I" with the circumstance to show how it is that through this fluctuation and uneasy relationship that exists between ideas and beliefs that the fusion of "I am I and my circumstances" occurs. For instance, one of Ortega's philosophical goals is to retain subjectivity in the face of the incessant and unyielding objectivity that is modern science. Furthermore, I will argue that in respect to the "problem of Spain" as he called it, there exists a further goal of retaining the vital past that Spain has in common with the traditional. But these values are opposed to the encroaching anxiety generated by the techniques of modern science as this pertains to the twentieth century. This was especially a dilemma for Ortega, since a great deal of his personal energy and attention was directed toward the Europeanizing of Spain. But the problem lies in that the modernizing of Spain could not be realized solely through the philosophy of convictions and personal beliefs. What then is the role that Ortega allots to ideas? This question is a central one in his thought. Indeed, the question arises of whether ideas and life are not ultimately contradictory and thus mutually excluding terms in his work.

Moreover, if man is indeed made of beliefs and can live an authentic life only by being true to himself as pertains to his convictions, what then is the role of ideas, and do we need them at all?[8] The first thing that must be said about Ortega's concept of ideas is that if beliefs are ingrained in us all, ideas by definition keep an objective distance from that "I" that defines us. This gulf that exists between my ideas and my "I" removes us from the "radical" immediacy and interiority that is man. This dualism Ortega manages to close somewhat, if not by rigorous ontological proof, then by a semantic inversion of sorts.

Therefore, what has hitherto been explained as subjective belief undergoes a dialectical movement in order to encompass what he describes as vital-reason as well. Vital-reason, seen as reason that springs from a vital need, pertains to man in his capacity as an organism, but it nevertheless falls short of theoretical and calculative reason, which is in effect pure reason. Such vital-reason can essentially be described as belief in reason. Belief now begins to count on reason as another manifestation of belief itself. Reason in this sense exists as a species of belief that is at the center of man. Man believes—has faith—in the intellect as a vital function, but not necessarily in ideas.[9] Ideas are secondary to living one's life because their sole reality belongs to the architectonic realm of conjecture or pure reason, while vital-reason is deeply embedded in the nature of man as a biological organism. In other words, Ortega views pure reason as a surplus of imagination that does not spring out of a vital necessity.

But in further developing this theme, let us look more closely for a moment at the overall direction that this dialectic of man takes. According to Ortega, we receive data or impressions passively from the external world. These impressions become transformed into beliefs that we embody. Some beliefs, on the other hand, do become ideas, and once that this epistemological metamorphosis is completed, we must no longer refer to our prior beliefs as beliefs, but rather as ideas. The key element that acts as the impetus for this change is itself a vital drive and never a theoretical one.

We see then that for Ortega the only way that we begin to theorize in the first place has everything to do with the essence of man. Part of the definition of man, as Ortega views him, is that above all, man as a vital entity is also a believer. Believer in this context must not be taken to mean belief in a transcendent God. To believe is to take our beliefs for granted prereflectively and to incorporate those beliefs in some fashion or form into our lives as vitality. But because man's nature is essentially to believe, not to know, he must consequently at times mistrust or doubt. This doubt, like belief itself, is a vital call for security or certainty and hence must not be interpreted to be what Descartes calls methodical. Instead, it marks the transition from mere belief to vital reason, which in turn will be the basis for theoretical reason.

Reason, then, for Ortega is born out of belief. It comes about through the gap that is formed in belief when doubt first arises. The same dialectical tension that exists between beliefs and ideas is to be found as a further split in the nature of beliefs themselves. When doubt breaks apart the unity and tranquility of blind beliefs, then doubt becomes a new belief in itself that will be antagonistic to the original belief that gave birth to it. Thus doubt becomes for Ortega the negation of stability.

When man finds himself at total ease with the security that his beliefs provide him, he has no need to develop or enhance his intellect as a vital function of his life. However, when doubt arises, there is a need for something more if life is to continue to grow. This something more is the intellect in the form of vital reason. Ortega has said that under the auspices of insecurity and doubt, the intellect is truly a "life-saver."[10]

This shift that is found in Ortega's notion of the breakup of beliefs, for example, is comparable to Maurice Blondel's notion of action, where action means a vital impetus for living, feeling, thinking, and willing that does not presuppose abstract thought. This similarity lies in the fact that both thinkers view action as a vital impetus, except that for Ortega doubt is necessarily a move toward individualization and concreteness. This is why, analogically speaking, according to Ortega, beliefs are to land as doubt is to water.[11]

Doubt as well as belief thus plays an essential role in Ortega's epistemology, since personal doubt will serve as the cornerstone of his critique of pure reason as a suspension of all belief in reason. Doubt, which is not intellectual or methodical, is part of our beliefs. When Ortega writes that "man is made of beliefs," this must simultaneously be read as meaning that man is always a doubter by his constitution.[12] Doubt, then, as part of our belief system, is not just something that we consciously entertain. Doubt expressed as a hole in belief is never an ideal that is planned in advance. Thus, for Ortega, we do not need to bring about doubt. Doubt is part of our human circumstance.

As with his understanding of beliefs, Ortega's notion of doubt is problematic because of the overall implications that it entails concerning his ethics. Doubt comes about when one finds oneself between two mutually exclusive beliefs that are furnished by the circumstance. The problem for Ortega's overall thought is that if belief is the natural and desirable state of man, it is not clear that he has shown that doubt and reason are not altogether antithetical to man's authentic state. To put it another way, if to find oneself in doubt in and of itself is in keeping with the nature of man, there seems to be no problem. But when this doubt is prolonged, then man according to Ortega is not living authentically given that man must have beliefs to sustain him. Concerning doubt, he writes:

> This is the moment to say that doubt, true doubt, the one that is not merely methodical or intellectual, is a mode of belief and thus belongs to the architecture of life.[13]

This thought has profound implications for Ortega's notion of *ensimismamiento* (authenticity) because it seems apparent that to leave the security of belief is also to lose something central to man's capacity to live fully. For this reason, at this point in our inquiry it becomes necessary to question to what degree is doubt itself a kind of belief. This is an essential question for our understanding the nature of belief, given Ortega's argument:

> In our beliefs our world is clear and explained. In doubt the world becomes ambiguous.[14]

Doubt opens up the door for reflective thought, especially when involving truth, which consequently shakes the foundation of beliefs.[15] The great paradox inherent in beliefs is that while holding them we do not question, that is, we do not doubt. But when we do begin to doubt, then we are forced to reflect in a hurry in order to find a belief in which to secure ourselves. Ortega's understanding of beliefs and his interpretation of truth is twofold. On the one hand, there is his insistence that the nature of truth is perspectival. But on the other hand, there is a sense in which he attempts to objectify truth. For instance, he states:

> When we walk through the streets we take it for granted that we cannot walk through buildings.[16]

But if we pay close attention to this statement, we must question whether this "taking for granted" is not really an affirmation of the truth. This is one instance in which "taking for granted" and truth are synonymous terms. The other alternative in this context would be to not take for granted that we cannot walk through walls. This would constitute an example in which the affirmation of a belief and truth are not synonymous operations. When a belief and truth part in different directions, as is quite often indeed the case, then a conflict ensues that manifests itself as anxiety or personal inquietude. To remove oneself from this state of uneasiness, ideas are sought. Nevertheless, these ideas do not necessarily convey the reality of the matter at hand. Ideas for Ortega move in a different direction from belief, but regardless, both are mutually subjective.

Both are opposed to the reality that is the external world. Thus, what is meant by ideas here encompasses the entire spectrum of philosophic, scientific, and religious thought.

The greatest dilemma that Ortega faces concerning his notion of ideas can be formulated as whether he can ground ideas in doubt, since doubt itself is born out of a hole found in belief. To put it another way: How can ideas, which are born from an existing hole in belief, be ideas of something real beyond belief?

This critique of reason is not a call to irrationalism, but rather an attempt to keep the status of man as a rational animal from becoming that of man as a theoretical animal. Belief is closely tied to Ortega's understanding of man as a historical being. Man as a rational animal, or as Jonathan Swift has put it so eloquently, "an animal capable of reason," is one who inherits history. History is inherited as beliefs that are passed on from generation to generation. The continuous chain of influence exerted upon our lives that constitutes history is suspended only when a belief is no longer taken for granted. Hence, when in doubt, reflect! Out of such reflection emerges an idea that will soothe our need for security. When ideas are embraced, according to Ortega, they become beliefs. In short, by believing in an idea, one already begins to see that idea as reality; therefore, that idea is no longer itself sensu stricto, but rather, it becomes a belief. He argues:

> In order that philosophy be born, life in the form of pure tradition must have become impossible; man must have lost "the faith of his forebears." Then the individual person remains isolated and uprooted, and nothing but his own exertion helps him to find new ground on which to settle new security. Only where this happens the extent to which it happens have we philosophy.[17]

Beliefs are dialectically structured, but in the final analysis the question of their relation to ideas and to reason can be settled by understanding that the nature of thought and consequently of human life is inward-directed or introspective. As we shall see, belief, so understood, is the ground for Ortega's idea of perspective as constitutive of life, which in his mature writings comes to mean human life as an individual life.

Part II Convictions: The Core of the Lived-Experience

Convictions = The state of being convinced; firm belief founded on evidence; the act of producing mental convictions; also a proposition which is firmly believed.[18]

Any epistemology that posits the human condition as consisting of man as radical reality, as Ortega does, must eventually pose the following two questions: 1) What ought I to believe? and 2) How must I live, given my beliefs? By attributing to man an urgent or immediate degree of reality, Ortega also tells us what his conception of man is. This view of man sees man as driven to fashion for himself a way of life that is founded on his beliefs. This urgency to "live" defines biographical man as a being who sees his life as a problem that ultimately emanates from within. This opens up the possibility that our private preferences come from a vital urge to "believe" and not from reason itself. Given that the original status of man is that of one who desires to believe through his constitution, the role of reason is dramatically deemphasized and redirected into the realm of the vital and organically functional belief. Therefore, belief is the opposite pole of pure reason, but it is not totally at odds with mere reason when the latter is seen as a vital cognitive function.

The effect of this is that Ortega goes as far as to turn ideas on their head so that it is through beliefs that we are grounded in reality. If this is the case, the more we place our trust in ideas, the more we remove ourselves from reality. It is our beliefs that keep us rooted in ourselves while ideas tend to devitalize and abstract biographical life, even though, in effect, ideas do have a direct line of correspondence with things-in-themselves. But what we call the world truly derives from our vital beliefs. Ortega makes this clear in the following two quotes:

> When we speak of the physical world, let us be warned that in its majority we do not possess it as the real world, but rather as an "interior imaginary world."[19]

Later he writes, "In my terminology, an idea in which man abides is called a belief."[20] But to say "an idea in which man abides is called a belief" is essentially to say that ideas are impotent as objective truth-bearers. Here we see the Humean skepticism that manifests itself throughout Ortega's thought. Husserl also expresses this same suspicion about rationalism when he writes:

> This great faith, which at a certain time took the place of religious faith and which believed that science leads to wisdom—to an actually rational knowledge of man, the world, and God and through this to a life ever capable of improvement, but verily and from the outset worth living a life in happiness, contentment, and well-being—this faith has doubtless lost its power in wide circles.[21]

Ortega cites this Husserlian notion of a great faith in reason as being a double-edged sword. On one hand, Ortega does seem optimistic about the role of reason as a tool for living. He views the sense of wonder of seventeenth-century man with enthusiasm when faith in reason as a tool for living is developed. As this belief became widely spread throughout the eighteenth and nineteenth centuries in Europe, it did seem possible that a pragmatic rendering of reason was indeed the philosophical turning point for modern man. On the other hand, the failure of this great faith, Ortega argues, is evident when it becomes obvious that the dictate of reason can only benefit man in resolving conflicts that originate in material causes.

The great faith, as Ortega would have it, must prove to be proficient and convincing in solving the problems of man that are of a philosophical and existential fiber if it is to be truly valuable to man. His formulation of this problem is in some respects paradoxical. First, there is his entire social-political project, which involves nothing less than the Europeanizing of Spain.[22] In other words, his aim was to modernize and upgrade Spanish intellectual endeavors, if not altogether Spain's self-identity, especially after the Spanish-American War. Obviously this project required an extensive overhaul of Spain's machinery and industrial productivity at the beginning of the twentieth century. One sign of this technical decay was Spain's defeated and irrelevant naval fleet by the turn of the century that saw the new age of the airplane and the steel naval destroyer. Certainly part of Ortega's integral plan of modernization involved the pragmatic rationalism and know-how of which America was the forerunner at the time. Given that he must have been aware of this, why then his disillusionment with the great faith?

Furthermore, given Ortega's original enthusiasm for vital reason and his distrust of pure reason, we need to ask whether he can reconcile these two views with the obvious need for applied reason that is needed in his overall program of revitalization. Our understanding of his critique of pure reason will enable us to conclude that this manner of reason is impotent and sterile when not employed in the service of individual life.

Perhaps a fruitful way to understand Ortega's critique of reason is by considering the emphasis that he places on *cultura animi* (cultivation of the heart) as opposed to pure reason.[23] This preference for all things pertaining to the heart—which are also equated with the will—first comes about as a reaction to the overabundance of faith in reason as showcased during the Renaissance by the likes of Descartes and Francis Bacon. This notion of the primacy of the will was first developed in Spain by Juan Luis Vives (1492–1540), known as Spain's leading Renaissance philosopher. Vives' philosophy of attributing primacy to the will over reason is known as *vivismo*. The word *vivismo* suggests the study of life *(vida)* itself. The emphasis of this doctrine is not that of asking "What is mind," but rather "What is the role of mind in human life?" This pragmatic line of questioning is quite clearly consistent with Ortega's emphasis of first living and later philosophizing.

Convictions, then, are the best example of *primum vivere duende philosophari*[24] whereby the dictates of daily life exhibit the *vigencia*[25] or vitality that is prereflective life. Convictions prior to religion, science, or reflective philosophical thought are our first line of defense against the objectifying force that is external reality. They are the end result of the subconscious dialectic that takes place among belief, doubt, and ideas. Convictions are, then, the root basis of human life, because our faith in rationalism dwindles when the essential problems of everyday life, be they social, moral, or spiritual, are not solved in spite of the fact, for example, that the medical field dating back to Hippocrates has improved man's overall quality of life.

Convictions, Ortega argues, solve the quintessential dilemmas of man by grounding man in life itself, which is the birthplace of all human problems. What religion, for instance, attempts to solve with faith in a transcendent God, and the socialist views as a problem of economics, and Camus as metaphysical rebellion, Ortega addresses as a problem of "faith" in the dictates of daily life itself. The totality that is individual human life manifests itself through our convictions. While cognition is seen as the capturing of being for the ancient Greeks, according to Ortega, this task is nevertheless bound to fail because life is the only reality that man can hold on to. This he believes to be the case because to look or search for something is already to possess or anticipate the being of that which we seek.

Convictions, in short, are the eternal enemies of rationalism because they are the affirmation of life, whereas rationalism in Ortega's estimation denounces life by abstracting it.[26] If man is to exist as radical reality, as Ortega has argued, then most certainly what keeps man as the focal point of reality is his network of convictions. Therefore, if we are to understand the makeup of man as radical reality, we must first see how convictions attempt to salvage subjectivity by asserting themselves in the life-world itself.

Part III The Affirmation of the Life-World

Perspectivism = Theory of knowledge; a metaphysics.[27]

Given that Ortega has downplayed the role of pure reason as pertaining to the vital aspects of man, what role then does he allot to reason, if any at all? As we shall see, what may appear to be an exaltation of irrational values is for Ortega nothing other than a "check" on the structure of absolute reason. More specifically, Ortega's critique of reason subjugates the demands of the objective world by giving primacy to the subjective immediacy that is man through the notion of perspective. It is precisely because of this emphasis on perspective, I believe, that his thought retains a taint of idealism. This residue of idealism in his thought, however, is not completely unexpected because, by attempting to move human life away from abstract reason, Ortega furnishes life with an inwardness and immediacy that necessarily gives primacy to subjectivity over the objective world. I shall return to this point in the final chapter of this dissertation.

To understand Ortega's conception of truth, it is first necessary to examine the dialectical process he employs. This aspect of his thought is less explicit than the dialectic underlying his account of belief and thus needs to be explained in some detail. He states that reason is one, absolute and invariable. Given this description, we might immediately develop a comparison to Plato's theory of forms. But a careful reading of Ortega takes us into an altogether different direction. Reason, he asserts, is what holds all mankind together. Yet it is not the case that there is a universal and absolute reason in which all of mankind partakes. Instead, what he means by reason is that all of mankind, as Jonathan Swift has said, is capable of the activity of reasoning as a vital function. Reason in this regard is not immutable and eternal, as Plato suggested; instead, reason in Ortega's view is always vital and personal, and only as such does all of mankind possess it in common. Nevertheless, a semblance of a Platonic strain is retained in Ortega's thought. For instance, Ortega refers to reason as being antihistorical because it cannot develop to its totality owing to the many obstacles and impediments that are placed in its way by history; for example, customs, traditions, the techniques characteristic of different epochs, and especially by human passions.

Thus, his notion of perspective creates a dualism or hierarchy of truth, one that is unattainable and another that is attainable, but only through individual perspective. The question of truth consequently is narrowed down to two possibilities: either truth is made manifest through rationalism, which must be consistent with objectivity, or truth has narrowed down what some critics have called a form of relativism by being rooted in individual life as perspective. Having seen his demand that truth maintain its objective immutability in spite of being splintered by man, it is difficult to view his understanding of truth as being that of relativism, as some have claimed.

For this reason Ortega cannot be seen as a complete relativist, given that he does not do away with truth altogether. Nevertheless, he is interested in dethroning reason and placing it at the service of life. But it remains difficult to understand how truth maintains its immutability if splintered by individual perspective. We get a clue as to how this can be from the following letter that Ortega wrote to Miguel de Unamuno, even though the letter was never mailed. In this letter, Ortega writes concerning the persona of Cervantes and the latter's concept of truth:

Marburg

February 10, 1907.

Cervantes views life as an absolute
Problem and he views all vital manifestation
In accordance with the final good (summum bonum)
Thus only infinity exists. What we call reality
is a deformation of the infinite. The world is a
spectacle; a moral spectacle. This deformation
takes place because of the plurality of points
of view.[28]

In this letter, Ortega sheds some light on his notion of perspective by arguing that all points of view are equally dogmatic, although this never leads to an absolute dogmatism such as he, for example, accuses Montaigne of espousing. He views the metaphysics of Cervantes as a metaphysics of imagination and perspective. Thus he views *Don Quijote* not strictly as literature, but also as a theory of reality that poses "reality as the individual manifestation of reality." Don Quijote and Sancho Panza are metaphorically two sides of the same epistemological coin. This is why in the persona of Don Quijote, Ortega sees a pessimistic metaphysics whereby all realities are tragic because none is real per se.

Reality, then, is not reality proper, but rather my reality. Thought, he will argue, is a process that hovers between subjectivity and objective truth. Nevertheless, the irony consists in that the individual attempts to convert his reality into objective reality. Furthermore, the dilemma lies in that Ortega's philosophical anthropology, unlike the whole of anthropology sensu strictu, attempts to find meaning in individual man and not abstract man since for him the latter falls short of being pure conjecture. Thought for him is a vital function that necessarily always pertains to individual life. Thus, thought becomes for Ortega a vitalistic element of personal survival.

Therefore, to think is to think the truth. This is the case because, according to Ortega, all subjectivity strives to think that which is true or what is good for it in fulfilling its respective function. His manner of connecting objective truth and subjectivity, and employing it in the service of life, depends on his belief that:

> Neither rationalist absolutism, which keeps reason but annihilates life, nor relativism, which keeps life but dissolves reason, are possibilities.[29]

This is why the task of avoiding a total refutation of reason and thus its invalidation, while at the same time exalting the values of personal life and vitality, gives rise to the central tension and decisive dialectic of his thought. Moreover, the argument that Ortega employs against idealism is the same argument that he directs against realism. Here we find that concerning this particular point, Philip Silver notes, "One could also say, a dialectical presentation of his own philosophy of vital reason."[30]

In downsizing the spectrum of reason to the range of what is vital for life, Ortega has no other recourse than to seek a fundamental aspect of man that can be defined, sustained, and grounded in life itself. The notion of man as vital reason is thus arrived at by a fusion of empiricism and vital intuition. In others words, the dialectical process by which Ortega arrives at his conception of man is essentially a movement from: 1) realism (thesis) to 2) idealism (antithesis), culminating in 3) I coexist with the world (synthesis).

I place realism as the thesis of this dialectic because we must keep in mind that Ortega views man as an entity coerced into reflection for his sheer survival. Man initially finds himself existing as an entity in a greater realm that is replete with other entities that act as resistance to his will. The external world, Ortega would argue, is our initial discovery. The discovery of the world acting upon our will is a prior discovery to the awareness of our mere subjectivity. This discovery in itself should be enough of an impetus to affirm and ground personal reality in the life-world. The reason that this is not sufficient in Ortega's estimation, however, is because the mere discovery of the external world is made possible through a silent and timid subjectivity that is awakened in the process.

As a consequence of this discovery, man is forced to reflect concerning his discovery of himself in this vast external world of which he is just another entity. This antithesis I have called idealism for two reasons, both of which are equally important. First, Ortega puts forth a great effort toward refuting Kant's notion of pure reason. This refutation of pure reason, I believe, is at least in part a reaction, as he has said, to the Kantian prison in which he was held prisoner for the duration of his stay at Marburg under the tutelage of Cohen and Natorp. The specific anatomy of this reaction, I believe, however, is due at least in part to his temperament as a thinker and a Spaniard. Let us remember that Ortega viewed autobiography as the best form of historical reason—that is, as self-understanding. While there may be some pertinent objections to this argument, we must also bear in mind that Ortega, even though greatly appreciative of Cohen as a teacher, nevertheless viewed him as "dry and somewhat of a positivist."[31]

Second, this refutation of pure reason grew into a reaction against the idealistic doctrine because Ortega viewed the latter as going against life itself. He interpreted the ancient Greeks as undertaking a scientific and synoptic analysis of life itself. This analysis of life is the greatness of the Greeks, as Ortega saw it, because it was not an analysis of thought thinking itself out. He saw philosophy for the Greeks as engaging in the pursuit of knowledge as a mode of living. This is precisely the same preoccupation that he views modern philosophy as lacking. The great turn comes with the thought of Descartes, who he viewed as turning his back on the problems of life itself. This is why he believed that in Marburg reality was not studied, but rather only Kant's terminology. Marburg's neo-Kantian emphasis, according to Ortega, remains a brand of the exact positivism that he saw as being antivital. Indeed, he even saw the neo-Kantian thinkers at Marburg as somewhat naive. According to him: "There is no knowledge, if not found through experience."[32]

The key words in this statement can be synthesized as "knowledge through experience." Knowledge through experience is open-ended and the culmination of the aforementioned tripartite discovery of the self. This open-ended relationship between subjectivity and the objective world makes man reflect by engendering a sense of doubt in himself. When Ortega states that beliefs are confused with reality itself, it is precisely doubt that he is referring to. In a sense, the self is encapsulated and thus protected by belief. This is why he views beliefs as constituting our world or horizon. Therefore, to affirm the life-world of our experience is to keep our beliefs from being withered away by doubts that are created as a product of a stifling objectivity. We get a personal indication of this notion from a letter that Ortega wrote to Unamuno from Marburg on November 3, 1906:

> It is the case that not having done a few favors in this life to other bipeds, I haven't a single friend. I do not think that anyone has ever placed more effort or more innocence in the search for friends. For years I have searched for another man that has had affinity with my animism. Useless. All of them have been too preoccupied with reality; all are always busy going somewhere. The characteristic thing about my animism is that I am outside of reality.[33]

To be outside of reality in this instance obviously does not mean the same as the person who is suffering from psychosis and who is not properly rooted in the reality that surrounds him. What Ortega espouses is the view that subjective inner reality and the objective external world are intrinsically at odds with each other and as such cannot be reconciled by pure reason. William Wordsworth perhaps best expresses this thought when he writes in "The World Is Too Much with Us":

The world is too much with us; late and soon getting and spending, we lay waste our powers: little we see in nature that is ours; we have given our hearts away, a sordid boon. This sea that bares her bosom to the moon.[34]

In working our way back from the culmination of the dialectic that is this tension between subjectivity and objective reality, we learn that this is precisely Adam's dilemma as much as it is of man as a whole, except that the problem is most genuinely approached from individual perspective. Ortega never rejects the objective world. Instead, he places man metaphysically outside of the world, as it were, and in this manner, it is said, "Man is in the world but the world is not in man." This is how man can genuinely affirm the existence of the reality that surrounds him without having to embrace such a reality to the detriment of neglecting his own existence. In this manner, man avoids making himself into yet another instance of an objective entity. This concern becomes the epicenter of Ortega's dualism between existence and genuine biographical human life.

To Live or to Exist?

Ortega argues that the moment that man comes into the world, his task is laid out for him clear and simple: How does he assert his subjective being in the material world? In other words, one needs to fashion a way of living for oneself. Ortega views this having-to-do that is man not only as inevitable but also as the foundation of what man as an existential being must be. This reflective strain is the basic stratum in the constitution of the being of man. Man is a prisoner of himself as an existential entity in a universe where, Ortega writes, "we are given no escape from last questions. In one fashion or another they are in us, whether we like it or not."[35] Ortega sees the greatest and most important questions as being those that are intrinsic to man.

The problem of defining man in Ortega's work is twofold.

This is the case because in one respect his critique of pure reason enables him to define man as a vital entity that is endowed with an organ whose sole function is to reason in order to live. But this problem also shows another face when Ortega argues that objective and immutable truth itself must also be salvaged from the wrecking ball of the material realm.

The true source of the dilemma of how to define man lies in Ortega's refutation of the rationalist notion of objective truth as merely diffusing itself through man as a passive agent. This to him is unacceptable on two accounts: First, because if this is the case, then man's faculty of reason is nothing other than an open-ended receptacle, much like the lens of a telescope, and thus not a vital reality. Second, because to allow man to come to know the totality that is truth would seem inconsistent with the limitation of man as a finite being.

However, to completely undermine the essence of objective truth wholeheartedly would allow reason to fashion reality simply to its liking or convenience. Ortega attempts to close this gulf by viewing vital-reason as a sieve that, when placed in the sea of objective truth, only manages to catch those aspects of truth that it can retain. Therefore man as vital reason is also man the selector:

> He does not allow himself, without more ado, to be permeated by reality, as would the imaginary rational entity created by rationalist definitions. Nor does he invent an illusory reality. His function is clearly selective.[36]

This manner of being as man the choicemaker is an affirmation of the life-world. This apparently simple and prereflective task that is based in man's network of beliefs is the quintessential difference between man and other merely biological forms of life. The totality that is man is all interior as opposed to a rock that is simply all extension. Man's affirmation of himself and his world derives from the possibilities that he possesses as life as narrative. Man therefore roots himself in the external world as this provides him with the arena in which to exercise the reality that he is as possibility. The external world allows for the realization of the possibilities that is man.

This Ortegan understanding of perspective is not readily evident and as such can be difficult to grasp. Therefore, I believe that a careful working through of perspective and vital reason as denominators of authenticity in his thought is required and thus we can now turn to this important point. He states many times throughout his work that man has no determinable being as denoted by the Hellenistic sense of the word. Thus when attempting to draw conclusions on how it is that man is defined as possessing a biographical life, as opposed to mere biological existence, it is not readily clear what role Ortega relegates to mere existence.

When man is busy deciphering what Ortega interprets as objective truth, given that he is an active reflective agent, he is also simultaneously creating himself. This Ortega clearly states in *The Modern Theme:*

> From the infinite number of elements which integrate reality the individual or receiving apparatus admits a certain proportion, whose form and substance coincide with meshes of his sensitized net. The rest, whether phenomena, facts or truths, remain beyond him. He knows nothing of them and does not perceive them.[37]

And what the form of this net is to truth in an objective manner, so too is our personal sensitized net is to personal consciousness. This selective opening to truth is the unique and central call of man, Ortega would argue. But it is precisely this definition of man that also forces us by implication to question how man must exist, and why.

If we begin with the premise that man has no being and "that man is not a thing, that it is false to talk of human nature, that man has no nature,"[38] it becomes clear that to speak of man's existence as such is nonsensical. Man as mere physical existence predicates

59

nothing about what man is metaphysically, except to say, as in the case of "I am," that as matter here and now, my being consists of simply taking up physical space.

But this places man in the dubious and uncomplimentary category of existence as is said of the rock, the crack in the sidewalk, or any of a series of bacteria that are said to "exist" on planet earth. If man is to exist and assert his existence as a metaphysical entity worthy of the title *Homo faber*, then existence as a mere substance will not suffice. In order for man to assert himself and create the history that will succeed him, the category of existence in Ortega's thought must be widened. To possess personal beliefs in and of their own right is already a manifestation of an entity effectively projecting itself outward onto entities, both alike and uncommon.[39] This strain in Ortega's thought of animating with reason what would otherwise be a mere vital organism can perhaps be traced to his discovery of and affinity for Aristotle's categories, which he discovered via Brentano's "On the Several Senses of Being in Aristotle."

Human existence by itself as a metaphysical cosmic phenomenon is not in itself problematic for Ortega in my estimation. All of Ortega's thought is: 1) an attempt at preserving the primacy of subjectivity and 2) showing why such a preservation is essential to a coherent concept of man in his philosophical program. His concern is rather one having to do with human values.

Man as Ortega has defined him can have no nature or being. But neither can he be said to merely exist-his-life, since that leaves him as pure exteriority or extension. The only viable option is for man to forge his own being, such that "to progress is to accumulate being, to store up reality."[40] Moreover, to assert himself as a vital entity in a universe replete with an endless array of entities, it becomes necessary that each man must be able to live-one's-existence.

To live, for Ortega, is to broaden the spectrum of existence from the crude and biological to the vital and existential where existence is the necessary hylomorphical background needed in order to create biographical and vital human life. To live is then necessarily problematical for Ortega because it is this category that engenders the possibility of choice, not biological existence.

But there is an obvious objection to this conception of man as living as opposed to merely existing that threatens the task of creating a philosophy of man. This objection can be articulated as follows:

(a) Given that man has no being, he therefore must create himself in his own image, as it were.

(b) But how is one to create anything coherently, much less one's own life, without a guide-plan? And of course,

(c) man has no direction since that which comes first in a series naturally has nothing preceding it.

In other words, Ortega, like later existentialists, has to make sense of the claim that existence precedes essence in regard to human life. Ortega manages to explain this only rather unconvincingly at first view, even though his more engaging solution, as we shall see, is part of his overall dialectic of man. This solution in his estimation is made possible by positing that:

> To begin with he [man] finds around him, in his circum-
> stance, other men, and the society they give rise to. Hence
> his humanity, that which begins to develop in him, takes its
> point of departure from another already developed, that has
> reached its culmination; in short to his humanity he adds
> other humanities.[41]

In effect, this collective notion of humanity that acts as a backdrop or guide map for personal choice and development is no other than history itself. Obviously this history is simply an aid to living and nothing more. Ortega would argue that those who simply follow the same path of history laid down by others before them have done so out of a vital choice because of their necessity to make something of their allotted time. This choice is a vital one, but the question now turns into one of authenticity for Ortega, a question we will take up in greater detail in the following chapter.

The last objection in creating essence for oneself can be articulated as: What about the first man, the one with no history, no humanity to guide him? In attempting to answer this question, Ortega's notion of belief plays a central role. This first man without history is Adam in Paradise, an entity who is coerced into existential reflection through a vital necessity. But this, as we have previously said, is the birthplace of beliefs. Thus the first man is sustained by beliefs that he has no reason or necessity to doubt. The anatomy of belief is such that only after finding some degree of comfort with beliefs does man take them for granted and therefore they become a species of habit. Adam is a metaphor for the first man, who finds that he must save himself quite literally, and only as a by-product does he create an essence for himself. In this way he affirms himself and his subjectivity vis-à-vis the external world.

Truth and the Anthropic Principle

> Conceive of a universe forever empty of life? Of course not; a philosopher of old might have said, contemptuously dismissing the question, and adding, over his shoulder, as he walked away, it has no sense to talk about a universe unless there is somebody there to talk about it.[42]

Ortega's staunch critique of reason can be said to restrict the meaning and scope of truth to the-things-themselves. Abstraction either in science or in dealing with human life is rejected in favor of the particular and concrete manifestations of individual entities. This aspect of his thought is due to the Aristotelian influence that he makes clear in *The Idea of Principle in Leibnitz and the Evolution of Deductive Theory*.

The emphasis of finding truth in the individual is the result of searching for a systematic phenomenon, which Ortega can only find in the individual vital life phenomenon. Philip Silver describes this analysis of vital man as an individual, as being Ortega's own brand of phenomenology because:

> For a systematic phenomenological thinking to be possible, it is necessary to start from a phenomenon that is itself systematic. This systematic phenomenon is human life and one must start with its situation and analysis.[43]

The systematic phenomenon that is man is truly the only measuring rod that Ortega finds valuable in confronting the problem of reality. To look outward for viable solutions in the fields of ethics, science, religion, or art is fruitless since the problem is human life itself. This anchoring of truth in life itself gives meaning to individual life, but only out of a necessity and not out of any correspondence with a transcendent truth to guide it. It can be argued that the relative phenomenon that time is to earth-based man in Einstein's theory of relativity, reality is to man according to Ortega. This being the case, according to Harold Raley, Ortega's vision of truth is restricted to individual man and as such:

> It is meaningless to affirm that it is "irrational" or that it is essentially "absurd" since first of all such assertions imply an absolute knowledge of the universe that man does not possess.[44]

The absolute knowledge of the universe that pure reason seeks both in philosophy and in modern science can achieve nothing other than disillusionment by removing man from himself. The only way to know truth is through individual perspective. But this, Ortega would argue, always falls short of the realm of objectivity. Man's only source of knowledge, then, is his perspective upon the universe:

> In the history of every living entity we shall always find that life at first is prodigal invention and that it then selects among the possibilities thus created, some of which consolidate in the form of useful habits.[45]

This entire critique of pure reason that Ortega espouses can best be explained today as the anthropic cosmological principle. This principle was first introduced by Brandon Carter in *Confrontation of Cosmological Theories with Observation* in 1974. The essential premise of the anthropic principle is that the existence of man in the universe as observer restricts to a great degree what can be expressed and therefore effectively limits what can be objectively known. The anthropic principle is in essence an epistemological position that limits what man as observer can know. This principle is actually composed of two principles:

1) The Weak Anthropic Principle
2) The Strong Anthropic Principle

The weak anthropic principle is an offshoot of the Copernican principle that shows how to separate the features of the universe whose appearance eventually depends on anthropocentric selection from among those features that can be determined by physical laws. The strong anthropic principle, on the other hand, in effect states that the universe could not have been structured differently, since we can only know a universe that we are biologically suited to know.

I have chosen to view Ortega's work as remaining in line with what has been a critical manner of questioning the epistemological limits of the scientific method. But what has Ortega to do with theoretical physics? When we look at the universe as an orderly system that appears to have a definite set of principles and formulas that lie at its core as its logos, we must ask where it is that these apparent laws reside.

The movement of the planets, the orbits of their moons, and the cycles of the sun, for instance, all appear to contain a structure that science can and does predict. Given then, that there is some semblance of order in the known cosmos, the question then becomes whether these laws are objective in themselves and, if they are, how can there be laws that no one recognizes? Or is it merely the case that these laws seem orderly to us who posit and thus recognize them? When we understand the problem in this manner, we discover that the problem is initially and essentially one of metaphysics and not of physics. The question that the anthropic principle poses is ancient in its own right, dating back to the pre-Socratics, when Anaxagoras attributed cosmic reason to the universe as Nous embraced the raw universe.[46] Thus, to consider this line of questioning as applicable to Ortega's work is one way of doing justice to a philosophical preoccupation that has been dismissed as unscientific since the advent and intellectual domination of the *novum organum.*

Stressed in this manner, the problems relating to idealism and realism are not to be dismissed as unscientific given that these problems are at the root of what it means to be human. Whether or not the laws of nature are objective as Newton emphasized, the reality is that man as an organism is endowed with sense organs that do in fact regulate the input of sensory experience that he undergoes. What is called the anthropic principle today by theoretical physics shares the same concerns that the Greeks had when science was not yet separated from metaphysics. In other words what the anthropic principle does is to philosophically question the limits of the scientific method.

Thus the need for man to create his own essence out of his mere biological existence, then, runs parallel with the weak anthropic principle's implication that the human aspects of life are separated from organic laws.[47] When Ortega writes, "Merely passing on a review of the film of our own lives reveals our individual destinies to be the result of the selection made by actual circumstances among our personal possibilities," he means that our perspective will determine our manner of confronting our possibilities.[48] The possibilities to which Ortega refers are indeed supplied by the perspective that one entertains, since individual perspective is man's only manner of piercing into truth. Granted that perspective is the manifestation of vital reason and not pure reason, one's perspective is always limited. Ortega goes on to say:

> The individual we grow to be in the course of our lives is only one of the many we might have been but had to leave behind—lamentable casualties of our inner army.[49]

These inner armies are our sensory faculties working on the features of the universe that require anthropocentric selection. The aging process, for instance, is indeed a necessary constant of nature. But the existential posture that man takes up as regards it depends on his ability to fashion his being in a manner comparable to such anthropocentric selection. Therefore, for Ortega the concept of belief coupled with perspective is meant to exhibit a teleology that aims at separating the purpose from the mere function of biological life. The purpose of individual life must not solely depend on what Newton referred to as the eutaxiological design argument, which states that order has a cause that is planned. In other words, the logos that operate the cosmos, in and of itself, is never a sufficient and convincing cause of individual life as meaningful. Like Aristotle, Ortega cannot speak of endowing the universe with objective meaning without first deciphering the final cause that motivates individual life. The greatest task that man must undertake is that of building an essence for himself as he lives. In learning to think and live, Ortega would argue that the task at hand is one where "in short, we must learn to disintellectualize the real if we are to be faithful to it."

The Physical Sciences and the Terrorism of the Laboratory: Subjectivity and Philosophical Knowledge

Science is closer to poetry than it is to our vital lives.[50]

When Ortega refers to the physical sciences as the "terrorism of the laboratory," his main concern is that the influence that modern science exerts over vital life subsequently abstracts life. This terrorism is nothing other than the result of physico-logico-mathematical *nuova scienza* that Galileo launched. At the center of Ortega's critique of pure reason inevitably lies his contempt for the quantitative and abstracting method of the physical sciences.

This particular aspect of Ortega's thought can best be understood if seen, as seems to be the case as well in the thought of Scheler and Husserl, as a reaction to the positivism that has ruled thought since the advent of Galileo's mathematization of nature. The concern that underlies this critique springs from the undeniable fact that since the age of Galileo mathematical physics has overtaken and thus undermined the task of metaphysics.[51]

This physico-mathematical reality, Ortega argues, is a direct consequence and construct of pure reason. The conflict thus is once again one between rationalism and reality. What Ortega means by reality is always rooted in the individual, so the ideal of a pure, universal rationalism becomes impossible. This is why Ortega rejects Spinoza's *species aeterna*. Frederick Copleston has the following to say concerning this point:

> The rationalist maintains that knowledge is possible only if reality can penetrate into the subject without the least deformation.[52]

Ortega clearly cannot embrace this definition of rationalism because it reduces men to replicas of each other and as such undermines individual autonomy. This is why Philip Silver argues that what Ortega calls perspectivism can be described noetically as saying that things are perceived as being "this or that."[53] What the physical sciences attempt to achieve is a total description and quantification of man that cannot be attained given that individual life is never qualifiedly either matter or spirit alone. Moreover for Silver, Ortega's notion of perspectivism means, "noetically that real things are aspectually perceived, that perception is "one-sided."[54] The reality that science proclaims must thus, according to Ortega's notion of philosophical anthropology, be seen as constituted by individual men, not by an abstraction called "man." This can be construed as a result of the influence that the thought of Scheler exerted over him.

The reality that science proclaims is according to Ortega a conjecture. If absolute reality exists, it must be only as pure conjecture, since only as such an abstraction can it keep from being fragmented by individual perspectives. However, even such pure reality is a phenomenon that can be grasped only starting from the individual, since no finite mind can possess the totality that is the infinite. Ortega's argument can thus be summed up as follows:

1) Reality itself is perspectival.
2) I see things through a given perspective, that is, partially; and
3) I take up (I am) a perspective; a point of view upon the universe.

The meaning that the laboratory conveys metaphorically is equivalent to removing life itself from the vitality that makes it dynamic, by abstracting it. What Ortega opposes is any such intellectualization of life. Vital-life is the entire organ that captures truth and that is rooted in reality. Reason cannot be abstracted from this vitality, which it must serve because life itself is the organ to which reality—even though partially—surrenders.

> There is no necessity to have recourse to extra-vital considerations, therefore theological, cultural, etc. Life itself selects and constructs its hierarchy of values.[55]

Chapter Four

Part I Vital Reason

My purpose in this chapter is to demonstrate that Ortega's philosophy of ratiovitalism necessarily retains an influence, if not a strong residue of idealism, and that this influence helps define his entire work, given his emphasis on the structure of life as radical reality.

Ortega's work fundamentally espouses the Heraclitian view that man is never what he is in his immediacy, but rather that he has to become what he is not through a self-conscious life project. The importance of this statement amounts to the critical setting up of his premise that man as a vital and existential phenomenon must be given primacy over the material world. If there is an essential and almost trivial difference, even though greatly neglected, between man and the material world, it is that while the rest of the world is already what it is as matter, man instead questions his existence as a vital entity among the things of the world. Things, Ortega has argued, are given their being already-made and as such they have no subsequent inner reality. Man, on the other hand, has an insurmountable degree of resistance against his existence, which furnishes him with the realization that he is an inner radical reality that is defined by this resistance as exerted on his will and aspirations.

But we must also question whether Ortega views man as radical reality because of the resistance offered us through our dealings with the world as circumstance. Or, can it be said that man is radical reality merely because of the phenomenon of being a self-conscious entity that can question itself regardless or despite of the circumstance?

The differences between these two possibilities are poignant and carry with them a number of philosophical consequences worth noting. For instance, if the former is true and man does in fact possess a radical and original point of view on the world that originates through his circumstances, then man is dependent upon these circumstances as an experience or force that reveals truth. In this instance, circumstance can be understood in terms of his rendition of truth as "that, which comes to us," which he espoused in 1914 in *Meditations on Quixote*.

But if the latter is said to be the case, then man as a self-directed and self-questioning phenomenon must be viewed as Ortega has defined him: as an extra natural phenomenon. Reading his work in detail, one gets the impression that it is man's distinct manner of being as phenomenon that makes human life the subject of existential analysis. In Ortega's hierarchy of being, man ranks as its zenith. As such, it is man's being that organizes and orients the lesser modes of being into the coherent and structured totality that appears self-evident to man.

Ortega's work can also be categorized as an incessant attempt to balance human life on the thin and fragile line that lies between the world of contemplation and that of action. The theme of intellectualism versus voluntarism comes about because, through the interplay of the two, Ortega is eventually able to ground his metaphysical anthropology in his mature thought. This fluctuation between thought and action is precisely the theme of *Man and People*, which he hoped would be his "most perfect" work.

A number of external factors come into play in this work that orient his thought in this direction. First, as we have shown, his thought is a reaction to his neo-Kantian schooling. Second, as we have also seen, he rejects what he considers to be the mathematization of nature as a static and lifeless construct of pure reason. Third, he saw the need to unify the Cartesian ego with the external world. To these, I believe that we must add that his Mediterranean temperament exhibits or adds a "sunny and jovial" quality to his thought that enabled him to maintain himself rooted in the common daily world of action. This point is not to be taken lightly, because while it deals less with logic or argument, it nevertheless has to do with the thinker as subject. This sense of Spanish practicality, for example, is also exhibited by Rodrigo (El Cid) Diaz's incessant readiness for action, by Sancho Panza's sense of reality, and by Miguel de Unamuno's reflection on death as being central to a proper understanding of life.

But nonetheless, while all of these factors may help guide his thought, it is Ortega's understanding of ratio-vitalism as a function of life that serves as the best tool to make sense of the balancing act necessary between thought and action. But as we saw earlier, man is radical reality above all because all subsequent realities are dependent on him.

If it can be maintained that man as radical reality is the hub from which all realities radiate, this enables man as radical reality to manifest his existence as the measure of all things. But isn't this the same as saying that the coherence of the external world depends on man? Ortega foresees this objection and counters it by saying that radical reality does not mean the first or the most important, but simply the central reality. But is it not also the most important one by implication and by virtue of its being the central reality from where all others radiate? For instance, Ortega would argue that the rings of Saturn or the Martian soil are not part of my reality, since they do not make up my everyday circumstance. He would nevertheless also argue that, to those scientists who specialize in the field of planetary astronomy, these two worlds do indeed constitute their circumstance and as such they are realities that are dependent on the being of the scientist qua radical reality.

But isn't this tantamount to saying that the extended entities that make up our circumstance, as the particular spatial-temporal mode of being that man embodies, can make their appearance known only through our subjective experience? If our circumstance, which initially appears to be an impersonal conglomeration of entities that make up the objective world, but that in greater inspection turn out to be unique and subjective, is equated with personal experience, doesn't this make reality purely subjective? And is this not the same thing that Kant meant when he wrote:

> We have sufficiently proved in the transcendental aesthetic that everything intuited in space or time, and therefore all objects of any experience possible to us, are nothing but appearances, that is, mere representations, which, in the manner in which they are represented, as extended beings, or as series of alterations, have no independent existence outside our thought. This doctrine I entitle transcendental idealism.[1]

It is logical to equate circumstance with experience if what is meant by experience is the totality of the events that make up our consciousness. However, when Ortega argues that every life is a perspective upon the universe, he does not negate objective truth. He merely states that man cannot know objective reality for two essential reasons. First, man is a finite being and as such he can know only that which enters into his consciousness at any given time, which incidentally means that which makes up his circumstance. Second, man as a finite consciousness rooted in time can engulf only a limited number of experiences, thus he is forced to make choices as to which to entertain and which to discard.

Man's subjective perspective can penetrate only as deep as the phenomenal level of the strata of reality. If man is limited by his subjectivity from arriving at a definite and objective realm of truth, it is because he lacks the tools to pierce into the noumenal realm beyond this phenomenal level, which Ortega never negates. But is this not reminiscent of Kant when he says that: "The objects of experience, then, are never given in themselves, but only in experience, and have no existence outside it."[2]

Seen in this regard we can say "I am and my circumstances" is essentially another manner of stating "I am I and my experiences." And if we grant that our circumstances are never identical, our experiences, then, are always personal even when others share them. Experiences in this personal sense are those things and events that occur to us as a radical reality. This individual and personal aspect of experience is an important point to emphasize, since Ortega's work always speaks directly to the particular and concrete and never to the universal.

Following from this, we can also see that existence is always also a process of volitional priorities, as is also the case with our perspective. To exist authentically is to be what I am, to embody this "I" self-consciously. That is, to state "I am I and my circumstances" is already to be self-consciously aware that one "is" an entity radically differentiated from all others. Ortega elaborates:

> Existence means, for each of us, the process of realizing, under given conditions, the aspiration we are.[3]

Therefore the things which are always-already-there are for Ortega a class of entities existentially radically apart from the phenomenon that constitutes the vital I of consciousness. He argues that things are only favorable or unfavorable in respect to us, but only according to our vital project. In other words, they are obstacles only if they are in the path of our volitional acts. Therefore, the question again arises whether man is the being that he is because of the resistance offered him by the world or if man is pure phenomenon, where phenomenon here is to be understood in the Greek sense of that which reveals itself to itself?

Part II *Alteracion* (Inauthenticity)

But Ortega is not overly concerned with this question in isolation. Instead, to him the real question is "How should man live?" The answer to the question concerning authenticity, as he views it, will eventually determine everything from our choice of religion, our manner of spending our time, our disposition toward others, and so on.

But the question concerning how man must live is the same apparent tension found in Ortega's theory of authenticity as exhibited by the apparent dichotomies that are at the core of his notion of ideas and life (action).[4] Ortega therefore attempts to reconcile the different perspectives offered by the terms "ideas" and "life," but the success of such an endeavor is not readily evident at first glance, as we will see.

The term life in Ortega's thought is synonymous with action, thus suggesting a degree of existential grounding in the world as pragma. But ideas, on the other hand, are indicative of a detachment that in Ortega's estimation is nonessential in the service of life. Nevertheless, his language concerning this point can be rather misleading. This is partly the case because most of his philosophy was initially presented in the form of newspaper articles or at public lectures aimed at general audiences.

Life, as we have stated, suggests a somewhat stoic attitude, but life cannot be entirely blind if one is to reinvent and conquer it every minute, as Ortega so often states we must do. It then seems appropriate that life, when authentic, must also possess a conscious guide-plan whereby the direction in which one is to move can be ready-known and thus foreseen. But in the process of acting one is also involved in the process of willing, and this willing must be directed. The alternative to this would be a model of action-reaction where one merely reacts to the dictates of the circumstance. This, then, could not be seen as "I am I and my circumstances" since my "I" would be engulfed by the circumstance. Thus the point being made here is that if nature and the circumstance are truly nothing other than resistance to our concerns, then one's commonsense choices are either: 1) evade the circumstance altogether in an act of inauthenticity or flight as expressed in Sartrean terms. Or 2) Modify our being to fit the circumstance. This possibility will eventually be deemed social adaptation, but it may nevertheless still highlight another phase of inauthenticity. A third viable possibility is to act blindly and with resignation in view of the circumstance as an obstacle, as in the case of, say, Taoism, since as Ortega has stated, the circumstance is only an obstacle according to one's project and therefore our perspective.

But this would also seem problematic because if circumstance is to be taken in its literal Latin meaning, then *circumstantia* is all of that which surrounds me. But how can that which surrounds me be a problem if I accept it wholeheartedly? Circumstance as experience is more appropriate to biographical life as problem, when negated, than is a mere description of it as that which surrounds us.

It is here where I think that Ortega's work recoils back into a brand of idealism that, while not absolute in nature, does nevertheless manage to ground the whole of life on subjective reflection. Viewed in this manner, it is life-as-phenomenon that properly depicts the dialectic of the inner-lived-experience that Ortega's work attempts to portray.[5] A close analysis of his rendition of the innate condition of man shows man to be a being whose fundamental mood *(stimmung)* is that of anxiety *(angst)*, as is for example, also the case in Heidegger's work.

It appears possible that if anxiety brings about the realization of our reality as a here-and-now, then the circumstance may play a secondary role at best. What my circumstance does is to circumscribe me, but it cannot be said to define me. While it is the case that Ortega views nothing as possibly existing in isolation, it is also important to emphasize that he also viewed circumstance as denoting my body and soul as aspects of my life that I must come to terms with. In other words, my life is my initial circumstance from which all others originate. It is my initial reality from which all others depend.

Given the nature of this structure of reality, man's foremost preoccupation is that of self-conscious interpretation of himself as phenomenon. Thus when Ortega writes that "the being of man presupposes action," the action of self-exegesis as an extranatural aspiration is sufficient to explain the being of man as an entity that by definition must live within himself as the radical reality that he is.[6] The other possibility, which is defined as blind action and thus inauthentic, places man outside or beside himself in the condition of an entity whose being is ready-made, as is the case pertaining to the being of the rock, vegetation, or animal life.

The notion that "I am I and my circumstance" taken in isolation does not exhibit the intricacies and antinomies that are the root of human life as radical reality. It is only after our understanding of Ortega's notion of inauthenticity, *alteración,* that a critical understanding of "I am I and my circumstance" can be achieved. The following quote from *Man and People* is a perfect summation of what Ortega views as inauthenticity:

> Almost all the world is in tumult, is beside itself, and when man is beside himself he loses his most essential attribute: the possibility of meditating, or withdrawing into himself in order to come to terms with himself and define what it is that he believes, what he truly detests. Being beside himself bemuses him to act mechanically in a frenetic somnambulism.[7]

From this statement we gather that the most basic tenet of inauthenticity is the state of "living outside of oneself." This, once again, becomes a problem only if we keep in mind that Ortega's task is to unify the being of man with the material world. The problem lies in that to find oneself living outside or beside oneself is to live according to the dictates of the circumstance. Under such conditions, the being of man is simply a material entity such as, say, atoms that mutually attract and repel each other. But this is not a viable position for Ortega to take, since he espouses the doctrine of ethical free will.

This is precisely the greatest weakness that his thought faces, I believe. He seems to be caught, on the one hand, between his intention of refuting neo-Kantian idealism and, on the other hand, his metaphysical anthropology notion of man as autodetermination. In unifying the "I am I" with the circumstances, he was refuting the positivistic influence that has dominated philosophy since the eighteenth century. This view he saw as a materialistic extreme that devalued and dehumanized thought. His goal in this respect is not to exchange human autonomy for a naturalistic and thus mechanical model of human life. However, regardless of this, he also did not want to isolate and thus alienate man from the material world.

Being beside oneself makes us into something that we do not choose to be. This state of existential exodus destroys the central (radical) possibility of man: that of meditating or withdrawing into oneself. This state of exodus can be said to be one of outward-directedness. This is precisely the literal meaning of the Spanish word *alteración:* a state of "otheration."

This state of total otherness or outwardness is best exhibited in animal life. But his environment, too, like the Simian at the zoo, harasses man. The difference being that Ortega argues that man can turn inward and detach himself from his surroundings, unlike the ape, which has a fixed being. Therefore, the essential dissimilarity between man and the other animals is man's ability to turn inward and negate both his physical and circumstantial surroundings.

But the greatest ambiguity found in Ortega's thought concerning this aspect of man is that he views man as naturally and therefore initially existentially caught up with the many entities of the material world. In other words, the natural posture of man is not one of thought, reflection, or meditation, but rather one of action, even blind action it can be argued. Thus turning inward into the self is, in his estimation, ironically an antinatural and antibiographical mode of being. Ortega has emphasized that man is an animal that first acts and only later learns to reflect in order to warrant his survival. This is why Ortega sees idealism as "one of the greatest sins of the last two hundred years."[8]

The question thus arises: Why does man turn inward in the first place? Granted that man's authentic being is that of *alteración;* of being beside himself as is the case of other animals. And then why is reflection not only needed, but valued? It obviously seems plausible that if man is naturally at home in his circumstantial surrounding, then to turn inward and cultivate an existential posture would seem to constitute a genuine mode of inauthenticity. Hence, Ortega then might argue that reflection is to man as the circus is to the performing Bengal tiger. Which then is the authentic manner of being a human being? This appears to be the central ambiguity in his work.

For Ortega, the life of the animal is always pure *alteración* through the sheer fact that the animal is not conscious of itself as animal. But if this is true, we must ask: How is it that the life of the animal is *alteración* if that constitutes its natural mode of being? The problem here can be formulated as follows: If the animal is said to live inauthentically, but also by the same token, it cannot attempt to turn inward because that is an antinatural mode of being, then what exactly is its mode of being? This would seem to be an absurd and moot point as far as the animal is concerned. *Alteración* is a natural condition in animals and not in man.

This is the same question we have raised concerning the ontological status of man in Ortega's work, I believe. Man's own coming face-to-face with himself can essentially be illustrated in three fundamental stages:

1) First, man feels himself lost as a shipwreck among things; this is the initial state of *alteración*.

2) Later, by an energetic effort, man withdraws into himself to form ideas and concepts about things and possible ways of dominating them. This is being within oneself, *ensimismamiento*, and the *vita contemplativa* of the Romans and the *theoretikos bios* of the Greeks; in other words, man now forms abstract concepts.

3) Last, man once again submerges himself in the world, to act in it, according to a preconceived plan, this is action, vita active, praxis.[9]

The central question in Ortega's work therefore has to do with man's initial state of being. Man, Ortega has stated, is an active entity. This being the case, there would seem to be little value in cultivating a contemplative mode of being given that, according to him, man reflects in order to survive and does not live merely to reflect. As he writes, "Man's destiny, then, is primarily action."[10]

Nonetheless, this apparent ambiguity lies in what I view as a basic indecision on Ortega's part. If he posits the being of man as originally consisting of action and only later beginning to reflect, this would constitute a move toward inauthenticity and not one toward authenticity.

But in essence what most often occurs throughout his work is that he views man as a naturally active agent who seeks authenticity through contemplation. This being the case, man then is indeed defined through his actions. Therefore, for Ortega, thought does not define man as swimming defines the fish. Man, he emphasizes, must learn to think while the fish does not need to learn how to swim. Therefore, he rejects Descartes' contention that man is a naturally thinking thing. The problem lies in that, in Ortega's definition of man as a naturally active agent, there must nevertheless be room made for a definition of man as at least a naturally "quasi-thinking thing," and not just one coerced into reflection. He writes:

> Because if for the present, in order to understand one another at this moment, we admit the traditional idea that thought is the characteristic of man—remember "man, a rational animal"—so that to be a man would be, as our inspired forefather, Descartes claimed, the same as to be a thinking thing—it would follow that man, by being endowed once and for all with thought, by possessing it with the certainty with which a constitutive and inalienable quality is possessed, would be sure of being man as the fish is in fact sure of being a fish. Now this is a formidable and a fatal error. Man is never sure that he will be able to exercise thought—that is, in an adequate manner; and only if it is adequate is it Thought.[11]

Here Ortega follows a line of thinking proper to an evolutionist where man gradually learns to reflect through the need for survival. Nevertheless, this does not detract from the fact that man is naturally endowed with the organ that enables contemplation, thus making man a thinking thing. In fact, I think that Ortega misreads Descartes by misinterpreting mere vital "thinking-thing" as "reflective thinking-thing." When Ortega emphasizes that man does not live to think but rather that he thinks to live, he means a species of contemplative thought that is closer in degree to conjectural pure reason than is Descartes' description of a naturally endowed, rational thinking thing. He further comments:

> Far from thought having been bestowed upon man, the truth is—a truth, which I cannot now properly support by argument but can only state—the truth is that he has continually been creating thought, making it little by little, perforce of a discipline, a culture or cultivation; a millennial, nay multimillennial effort, without having yet succeeded—far from it! in finishing the job.[12]

Here one would think that Ortega is arguing for a model of man as a rational animal, given that he sees thought as an evolutionary process whose effectiveness has not yet been maximized. Yet if Ortega indeed espouses the view that the destiny of man is primarily action, it becomes difficult to understand the preceding quotation where he argues that man has not quite realized the potential of thought.

Does his position, then, not presuppose an objective standard of thought? If man is an active agent, who is then to say what the limits of thought are? This argument sounds as if Ortega is arguing for a notion of authenticity that is rooted in contemplation and not action. But this is not what he means when he writes, "While the tiger cannot stop being a tiger, cannot be de-tigered, man lives in perpetual danger of being dehumanized."[13]

What Ortega implies here by "being dehumanized" is the ability for self-conscious contemplation and therefore reflection. But, if man's humanity has been acquired gradually through reflective thought, which in itself, according to Ortega, is an unnatural activity to man, how can being dehumanized be an imminent danger?

The vagueness if not uncertainty underlying Ortega's argument can be traced back to the definitions of what he understands by action and thought. It is my contention that if Ortega argues for a model of man as originally an active agent prior to any and all reflection, then it becomes difficult to understand his overall view of man as a free choice-maker. But, on the other hand, if what is meant by action is originally accompanied by some degree of self-conscious thought, it then becomes clear that man must indeed possess a guided and willed plan of action in understanding himself as phenomenon. The latter of these options must be the case if we are to take seriously Ortega's notion that: "Ignorance is, in fact, man's privilege. Neither God nor beast is ignorant—the former because he possesses all knowledge, the latter because he needs none."[14]

But let us be clear that what he means by ignorance is a "conscious ignorance" in the sense that man chooses what to know, like learning to study Renaissance history as opposed to, say, ancient history. Thus it can be said that man's ignorance is in part a negation of knowledge. Let us imagine, for the sake of argument, Socrates as attempting to learn the techniques of pottery-making instead of trying to know himself as a way of life. This conscious and discriminating sense of ignorance is a sign of man as a thinking thing, since this description of ignorance is contingent and therefore determined by circumstance. The animal, on the other hand, is ignorant through a lack of vital capacity to know. It cannot choose what to know. This is an example of pure action, of being totally immersed in the circumstance, and therefore this cannot be regarded as ignorance.

For this reason, Ortega writes that ignorance is a luxury that only man can enjoy due to the fact that God is omniscient and the lower animals are totally "ignorant." This definition of ignorance is symbolic of an entity endowed with self-conscious thought by virtue of its constitution.

It would appear that if it is both the privilege and destiny of man to become lost within himself, as Ortega has written, then it would be appropriate to think that man is an alien to himself while immersed in the world or circumstance. The only saving grace or avenue open to man, then, is to turn inward and move away from the spectrum of the merely instinctual animal level. Thus, if the notion of inauthenticity is to be a philosophical problem, it must be understood as a movement from a genuinely existential inwardness that is uniquely human to an outwardness that dehumanizes and enslaves man to the dictates of circumstance. Moreover, without "this radical reality, on the strict contemplation of which we must finally found and assure all our knowledge of anything," there would be no circumstance and its absence would inhibit the usage of action as the offshoot of a being that is uniquely an extranatural aspiration.[15]

It is precisely owing to this fact of man being a thinking thing that Ortega can speak of human life as follows:

> This inexorable genuineness of our life, the life, I respect of each one of us, this genuineness that is evident, indubitable, unquestionable to itself, is my first reason for calling our life radical reality.[16]

It is human reflection and not just vital thinking that is the issue for Ortega, since to merely speak of man as an inauthentic entity capable only of action would be a logical flaw given that only an entity capable of formulating a concept of inauthenticity is capable of reflective thought. Ortega emphasizes this point, even though somewhat vaguely, when he writes:

> The circumstance, I repeat—the here and now in which we are inexorably inscribed and imprisoned—does not at every moment impose on us a single act or activity but various possible acts or activities, and cruelly leaves us to our own initiative and inspiration, hence to our own responsibility.[17]

This apparent ambiguity is worth noting because it is a central aspect of his philosophy. On one account, we are told that the circumstance "inexorably inscribes and imprisons us," but later we are told that the circumstances also "cruelly leave us to our own initiative and inspiration." Here we must question: How does the circumstance act upon us if we are free to act in the final analysis? Or is it possible that the circumstance acts on our will through a negation? That is, the world does not explicitly tell me how to act, but rather what not to do, therefore forcing me to choose.

It is important to realize that my objection to this aspect of Ortega's thought is not that he does not see the possibility of man making an inward turn, because this much he does say. My main objection derives from my interpretation of Ortega's understanding of the original state of the being of man, because only in this way can an appropriate understanding of authenticity be reached. For instance, Ortega attributes the state of moral decay of Europe in the first half of the twentieth century to man's "seeking to flee from all taking a stand within the self and to give themselves up to the opposite extreme."[18] The opposite extreme here would be a state of pure action or a voluntarist state of being outside of oneself. This state of pure action followed from what Ortega considers the intellectualist aberration that isolates thought from life. This difference is very important in not only understanding Ortega's notion of authenticity, but also how this relates to man as a social entity.

The question remains, however, whether man as radical reality is the authentic state of being of man or if authenticity is an acquired but unnatural state of consciousness? He states concerning life as radical reality: "that it is the root of all other realities, in the sense that they—any of them—in order to be reality to us must in some way make themselves present, or at least announce themselves, within the shaken confines of our own life."[19]

Moreover, any mode of being that manifests itself as radical reality, as a unifying point of reference for objective reality, as is said of man, must exist authentically as such. The alternative is to view man as gradually becoming a radical reality in accordance to one's respective degree of contemplation. But if this is the case, who is to say when this task is either commencing or if it can ever be completely achieved. Moreover, who is to judge when such a dynamic and infinite state is completed, as is said of self-actualization, if the latter is proportional to one's level of reflection? It would make more sense to argue that man exists and must exist as radical reality if he is to be self-conscious at all. This is the inherent difference between man as a naturally thinking thing and man as a reflective thinking thing.

Also, if man is to exist authentically as radical reality, receiving and interpreting sense data from the circumstances in order to maintain himself alive, as Ortega has argued, he must do so as a detached and self-conscious being. This must be the case, since one is responsible for choosing how to act, given that the circumstance appears only as an imposing impediment and never as a readily available solution. This being the case:

> [man] has to choose and decide for itself, untransferably, for itself and before itself upon its own sole responsibility.[20]

The kind of being of which Ortega speaks here exhibits an innate ability to question itself vis-à-vis the world. And what is man's best tool for undertaking such a task? Reason, of course. In a manner of speaking, it can be said that it is imperative that the being that man is confronts itself in this fashion with the world at large in order to survive. But mere survival carries with it a heavy existential burden. Through this interaction, man loses himself in the world, becomes part of the world, it can be said, and thus comes to live outside of himself. Yet any being that must concern itself with the world for its survival and that maintains itself aware of such a reality is necessarily simultaneously abreast of the inwardness that it possesses. Ortega's notion of inauthenticity becomes clear if one keeps in mind that *alteración* in Spanish comes from the Latin *alter*, or to turn one's being inside-out. But if to alter, or as Ortega has said, "to otherize" one's existence is an undesirable state of alteration, then can a total withdrawal from the world in the manner of *ensimismamiento* be a valuable alternative if a mediation between thought and action is the desired goal?

To live an authentic life, then, is to "live within oneself," but to do so without totally abandoning the world. This turn inward acts as man's salvation in order to keep him from being overburdened by the circumstance. From this state of consciousness, man can cultivate a panoramic view of existence and thus make conscious choices. While Ortega finds this a valid description of one phase of the authentic life, he also refers to this mode of being throughout his work as the core of intellectualism. The desired balance between a life of action and one of contemplation, he argues, is achieved through the respective stages of the dialectic that is exercised in the resistance offered by experience to one's willed aspirations.

Therefore, the life of the reclusive Buddhist, Stoic, or early Christian ascetic desert dweller all appear to be examples of an authentic existence on one face of this argument. The problem is that inauthenticity in Ortega's estimation manifests itself in either one of these two poles. Thus, the contemplative life showcases a particular brand of inauthenticity while the grossly pragmatic life is the other face of inauthenticity. The problem seems truly provocative if we examine the two poles of the life of Marcus Aurelius, both as emperor-philosopher and later private philosopher citizen, given that the substratum of substance that is the being of Marcus Aurelius never changed, but rather only the outward manifestations of such a life.

Part III *Ensimismamiento* (Authenticity)

When understood as extranatural phenomena, man must also be seen as a natural doubter. As a questioning being, man must necessarily take command of his life in opposition to the dictates of his circumstances. Ortega's notion of authenticity is truly another possible word for subjectivism, if understood as a means toward the renewal of thought qua metaphysics. For instance, I have heard that 2+2=4, but Ortega argues that one must figure out this truism by oneself. Through personal reflection the essence and therefore truth or falsity of such a statement becomes genuinely authentic. This is why Ortega views truth as dialectical and perspectival. But does this not also amount to a reinventing of the world over and over again? And doesn't this attitude resemble solipsism by taking nothing on blind faith? Consider the following statement by Ortega: "Human life is, in the strict sense, untransferable. It is essentially solitude, radical solitude."[21]

This solitude consists precisely in one's having to face the experiences engendered by one's circumstances as personal and their immediacy as intersecting one's being. The anatomy of this intersecting of our being with "our experiences" is best understood as the phenomenology of our being as it moves through the field of possibilities that is the world. What amounts in retrospect to constituting "our" experiences is in essence this dialectic at work. Thus the ebb and flow of being as it moves through the material world creates the illusion of logical laws, when it is more than likely that these illusory laws are merely the product of our will.

Following this argument to its logical conclusion will enable us to make sense of Ortega's definition of authenticity. A being that is alone is for Ortega necessarily a being self-conscious of his own existence. By no means does Ortega attribute physical existence only to man alone as phenomenon, given his concern with solipsism. Ortega understands man as understanding himself to exist in a universe replete with objects and other beings. Therefore, man is never physically alone, but rather literally surrounded by the universe, if we understand this in the sense of the special theory of relativity whereby anywhere that one finds oneself can be designated as the center of the universe.[22] Life as radical reality, then, enables man to feel as a necessary stepping-stone in the "supreme unity" of all things that characterizes Spinoza's "intellectual love of God." Ortega explains:

> The radical solitude of human life, the being of man does not, then, consist in there really being nothing except himself.

Quite the contrary—there is nothing less than the universe, with all that it contains. There is, then, an infinity of things but—there it is!—amid them man in his radical reality is alone, alone with them. And since among these things there are other human beings, he is alone with them, too.[23]

As we have seen, Ortega places man as the center of a perplexing and challenging universe in an attempt to keep man from recoiling back into himself in the form of solipsism. This is Ortega's main line of defense against idealism. But what form or degree of idealism does he refute is the question. This question is a central one in his work because it must not be said that Ortega is a commonsense realist. But as previously stated, Ortega equates idealism with a conjecture of pure reason, and his main refutation of idealism has to do with it as epistemology, not as ontology. This is why, even though he rejects Descartes for his splitting of mind, and body and Leibniz's notion of the monad for being locked up in itself, he nevertheless still grants the primacy of self, mind and spiritual values over the material world. It seems appropriate, therefore, to view Ortega as being closer to the Kantian notion of a transcendental form of idealism than he is to Descartes' "problematic idealism" or Berkeley's "immaterialism." For instance, when Ortega writes "everything that composes, fills, and makes up the world in which man finds himself at birth possesses no independent condition of itself, possesses no being of its own, is nothing in itself—but is simply something for or something against our ends,"[24] he clearly places man at the zenith of the hierarchy of being and as the measure of all things. This is the logical conclusion, I believe, of positing man as radical reality. While man as radical reality is not the sole reality, he does necessarily become the central reality.

Ortega thus appears to be saying that a choice has already been made as to how to confront the world, and therefore our ideal of the world cannot become completely clouded by our circumstance. In *Notes on Thinking*, he then appears to share Kant's view more so than his comments at first view may seem to imply.

Reality, as Heraclitus already observed, likes to hide. The world is a constant carnival. Masks surround us. Forests cannot be seen for trees, trees for leaves, and so on.

This passage directs us to a definition of authenticity that is nothing other than that which is self-consciously willed. Thus, whether man is physically alone in the universe as a solitary being or whether he is surrounded by other entities, the question still remains as to whether the constitution of man is to be alone within himself. As he writes, "alone, and that only in our solitude are we our truth."[25]

The world as a secondary reality or, as Ortega describes it, as pertaining to the second degree of reality, always remains outside of us as a reality that is not what constitutes our inner life. The world in this respect is alien or foreign to us. Even though the world is made up of our spatial-temporal circumstance as our material reality, it nevertheless does not set our existential precedent for living. Physical things in the world as well as emotions and thoughts, Ortega has said, are our concern for living only if we allow them to define our life. But isn't a concern already at the conscious level also an idea?

The many things of the material world, then, as static entities have nothing to do with me, but I, on the other hand, have to deal with them. But the reason that they have nothing to do with me is because of their lack of consciousness. Self-conscious man, on the other hand, must reckon with them as entities that occupy our consciousness. Therefore, is not man's sole concern then the problem of consciousness, and especially when concerning self-consciousness? Assuming that this is the case, what then is the constitution of the world-as-circumstance? If self-consciousness is the greatest contributor to the possibility of human authenticity, what then is the relationship between Ortega's first person conscious "I" with the circumstance?

To put this in another way, in the process of working out "I am I and my circumstance," isn't the personal "I" already asserting itself as a self-conscious phenomenon when confronted with the circumstance? Granting that this is the case, isn't this an introspective and contemplative position and thus not truly one of praxis? The other alternative is to live "outside" of oneself as the animal does by solely concentrating on our environment. But even this latter possibility, as we have seen, is not too remote from Ortega's understanding of authenticity as the natural state of man.

I would conclude therefore that if Ortega's metaphysical anthropology is to be convincing, we must arrive at the realization that it can only be so by positing human existence as a subjective self-conscious, as a radical reality, and not as merely a pragmatic being. It is best to view this rendition of authenticity as being a copresent state of being where something that is not present (perpetual self-conscious thought) is united with that which exists as pragma. Thus we have Ortega's notion that human thinking is only humanly valid when it is done on my own account. In other words, I must be consciously aware of it. This is why, for Ortega, only from radical reality can all realities be possible. Therefore, he uses the metaphors—appear, dawn, bud, arise, and exist—to describe how all subsequent realities depend on personal radical reality.

To conclude this chapter, then, I must reiterate my contention that Ortega's taint of idealism is categorized as an inner reality that understands itself as possessing an innate awareness or ignorance of itself, as the case may be, when confronted with the world. Thus Ortega writes: "Environment is the part of the world that at every moment comprises my horizon of vision and that therefore is present to me."[26]

The circumstance, then, forces us to turn inward and view ourselves as the subject to the resistance that is the world. The world, then, can exist because of man. Man is the reference point for the reality of all things.[27] Therefore, existence must be conquered literally minute after minute in a perpetual program of conscious self-assessment, and only as such can it exhibit primacy over the world.

Chapter Five

Ortega's Philosophy of History

> In order to encounter authentic reality in its sheer naked-
> ness we would have to remove all the layers of today and
> yesterday's beliefs, all of those theories that are nothing but
> interpretations thought up by man about what he finds in
> living, in himself, and in his milieu.[1]

The first section of what is today published in book form under the title *Historical Reason* was originally offered as a series of five lectures given at the faculty of philosophy of the University of Buenos Aires, Argentina, during October 1940. The second sec-tion of this book is composed of another five lectures that Ortega offered, but this time at the faculty of philosophy of the University of Lisbon in Portugal during 1944. Thus one section of the book is *Historical Reason* (Buenos Aires) and the other is known as *His-torical Reason* (Lisbon).

The point to be made in these ten separate lectures is the contention that "the fate of western man and the world he has built was conditioned to a great extent by the kind of thinking practiced by the philosophers of ancient Greece."[2] The kind of thinking that Ortega is concerned with is specifically Eleatic reason, which equates thought with reality, as is the case with Parmenides. Therefore, the connotation that underlies *Historical Reason* is to be understood as a signpost that both dissects as well as offers a new course of direction for Western thought.

The striking thing that may first puzzle a reader not well acquainted with Ortega's thought is that this work is neither a work of history as a chronological study of events, nor is it a philosophy of the architectonic of past events in the manner of Arnold Toynbee, for instance. In order to address Ortega's philosophy of history, it is necessary to consult the following works: *History as a System, An Interpretation of Universal History,* and *En Torno a Galileo* (translated as *Man and Crisis).*

Historical Reason itself is an analysis and also a diagnosis of the moral and existential condition of man and a prescription of what direction should be taken in the West as a corrective to this precarious moral condition. This work offers, in Ortega's estimation, a new metaphysical basis to the course of direction that the West must embrace if it is to take seriously its own moral condition. What he attempts to achieve amounts to a leveling of the historical infrastructure in hope of addressing and redirecting the essence of metaphysics as: human life as first philosophy.

Even though in the quotation cited at the beginning of this chapter Ortega views history as a series or strata of interpretations that have accumulated over the years beginning with the Greeks, his main and immediate concern has to do with his critique of Descartes' metaphysics. In order to define and therefore understand what Ortega calls historical reason, it will be necessary for us to set up the problem as he saw it, for this problem renders possible his call for historical reason as necessary.

First, there is the Greek and medieval notion that the "world of things" is primordial reality.[3] This, as we have seen, in Ortega's estimation constitutes a naive and gross rendition of reality that detracts from the reality that is the self qua self-consciousness. This in Ortega's estimation showcases the worst possible example of inauthenticity because it completely takes for granted the immediacy and intimacy that is human life.

Then there is also his critique of Descartes, whose project he views as overzealous and thus as polarizing consciousness, if not all of reality, into two irreconcilable spheres. These opposite poles are constituted by Descartes' contention that being and reality are not independent of consciousness. Hence for Descartes, primordial reality is the cogito or thought. This, Ortega thinks, leaves man paralyzed as an inactive agent immersed in a nonmaterialist unreality without a vital arena to move in. Therefore, for Ortega the question became: What is the most adequate term or designation for the primary relationship of man with things?

Returning to our opening quotation, we can pursue this question in terms of the further addressing of the question: What is Ortega's alternative to a history whose sole nature is an accumulation of interpretations? We need also to ask: How is one to proceed in living, if not by accepting some fundamental principles on faith? The logical conclusion of this assumption, as we have previously mentioned, would render man simultaneously an eternal builder and destroyer, given the belief that he must destroy the preceding truths in order to make room for his own. This is in a certain respect indeed the case in history, literature, philosophy, science, and art evidence in Greek architecture with the invention of the *tholos* or round building. It also applies to Da Vinci's radical inventions: his pioneer spirit in his rendition of the techniques of linear perspective and *sfumato;* as well as to Michelangelo's technique of fresco painting and the Wright brothers' reinterpretation and thus their realization of the myth of Icarus and Daedalus with the invention of the airplane.

Historical reason so understood is Ortega's understanding of life as a dialectic that is made possible through thought, will, and the circumstance. Therefore, historical reason is the quantitative result of the existential dialectic of the self. Thus what is meant by historical reason is to be interpreted as man's moral existential mark upon the world. Moreover, historical reason is, in Ortega's thinking, a vital mode of capturing and deciphering reality that asks of us only that which we are prepared to offer. In other words, we can battle reality only in our own personal terms and according to our own existential capacity.

Given that historical reason so conceived is the logical offshoot of vital reason, history indeed becomes a collective stratification of *doxa* that initially begins as a vitally original and personal impulsive retreat into the self. Any original creation, Ortega argues, is a retreat into the self, even though this impulse should originate from within and not from the circumstance. Thus, the authentic life is one best understood as anabasis. Plato tells us:

> —and here Plato's unruly disciple Aristotle agrees—that philosophy is, in his formal definition, the science of free men. Or to translate it so as not to lose the nuance the word had in Athens, the science of noble men.[4]

This offers us a definition of philosophy as retreat, but how does man become free to attempt such a retreat? Can this be achieved by a total immersion into the self while withdrawing from the world? Or is it necessary to take full account of the circumstance as a preparation to retreat? These are all pressing questions, since one must not forget that Ortega refers to his thought as being circumstantial. Authenticity as genuine anabasis, Ortega stresses, cannot be achieved by a mere desire to be original, but by a vital constitution that knows no other manner of being. To this end he writes:

> To realize or be aware of something without counting on it is the most characteristic form of an idea; to count on something without realizing it, is the most characteristic form of a belief. Here, then, are two distinct modes of human comportment.[5]

Thus, the authentic life is to be identified with contemplation, reflection, and truth. But authenticity is also characterized as an openness to truth. That is, truth speaks to us through the dialectic that is our lived experience. For this reason, for example, *Meditations on Quixote* is a study of the different stages of truth made known in personal life. The reference to Don Quixote is merely an allegorical tool that enables Ortega to set up this problematic. To this end he further comments:

> Throughout the world people are engaged in frenetic activity, drugging themselves with inauthenticity in order to fill the vacuum of not knowing what to do; and at the other end of the scale is the complete-do-nothings, with their attitude

of quiet desperation, of self-abandonment to the rushing course of events.[6]

From this, one gathers that authenticity is a state of inner tranquility that is the opposite of inauthenticity, which is best expressed as hyperactivity. This hyperactivity in turn is best defined as a detachment from oneself due to one's being held hostage by the commands of the daily world. Authenticity, on the other hand, is defined as a state of being attuned to one's inner self. This inner self-awareness can also be described as the ability to be free, as when Ortega writes about Plato and Aristotle's notion of philosophy.[7]

Freedom Ortega equates with reflection, through taking nothing for granted. For instance, our circumstance cannot determine man's action because it is man's responsibility to interpret it and then proceed according to our own rational dictate. Ortega's manner of rejecting the view of material reality as primordial reality finds its absolute opposite in Descartes' primacy of the cogito over the material world. This Ortega makes clear in the following quotation:

> My being aware of this room, according to the modern idealism of Descartes, means that its image but not the room itself is present to me.[8]

Ortega, on the contrary, sees freedom as a metaphysical reality that is evident through the friction that is created in our dealings with our circumstance. That is, freedom is denoted by reflection in the sense of Socrates knowing the world through a prior commitment to know himself. Ortega's notion of freedom as metaphysical is interesting because this is the substance of all of our subsequent dealings with the world. This is why his task is one of a return to first philosophy, since nothing else can be achieved without a prior understanding of this essential category of human life. This is why his thought does not quite arrive at a full-fledged analysis of politics. His questioning is instead always directed to the metaphysical underpinning that exists prior to the manifestations of the worldly reality that is politics.

But Ortega runs into a deeper obstacle by attempting a synthesis of naive realism with self-conscious reflection. Where before our discussion asked whether man acts blindly without prior reflecting or whether he reflects and does not act, now, we see that Ortega views reflection as a willed activity that is never spontaneous. This line of thinking he undertakes in order to refute Descartes' notion of consciousness as well as Husserl's, even though his refutation of the latter comes about indirectly. He writes: "But this active decision is by no means theoretical, but an act of will. Descartes resolved to do philosophy because apparently he needed to do something to exist, to subsist and because that something was theorizing."[9] What Ortega rejects is Descartes' claim to the immediacy and primacy of thought, and therefore he negates the notion of spontaneous reflection, based on the grounds that to reflect already presupposes a previously made decision to theorize. But isn't it the same thing to think that one is going to reflect and the fact that one is already reflecting? By engaging in this line of thinking, Ortega not only negates the primacy of the cogito, he also exalts the notion that in thinking we only react to our circumstances and thus we again arrive at "I am I and my circumstances." He even goes as far as using Descartes himself as an example of one who reflects out of compulsion. He views Descartes as an example of one who consciously decides to reflect due to his circumstances. This is important because Ortega would not agree that Descartes' thought is spontaneous, but rather that it is a theoretical construct. Ortega argues, for instance, that when I see a dog, I see only the dog and not simultaneously my seeing the dog. My seeing the dog is a spontaneous act of my prereflective consciousness. This is why his understanding of man as radical reality can be said to be limited to an action-reaction model of behavior. In essence, the vitality that constitutes life for Ortega is always prereflective, whereas his notion of consciousness refers to that which:

is supposed to be a reality that is aware of itself, something immediate to itself, pure reflexiveness.[10]

This notion of consciousness Ortega thinks should be banned from all philosophical inquiry. Instead, consciousness, he has argued, is not capable of self-questioning in its stage of immediacy, but is rather more like an open receptacle. However, I would add that in the process of prereflective thought, one's initial reality, nonetheless, by implication continues to be of ourselves by virtue of our having to deal with our circumstance. This I believe to be the case since our material circumstance is physically detached from our conscious I. But given Ortega's views, it seems difficult to interpret his notion of authenticity to mean a more or less uncritical natural attitude of beliefs, which are used for the purpose of living. But how then can one remake one's life and avoid a "piling" up of opinions, if to reflect is to theorize and to theorize is already an autofabrication of man? A possible is that Ortega does think that man should exercise his freedom to question the opinions that make up his circumstance and therefore live authentically. Yet this can be misleading because, while this indeed is the case, what Ortega views as thought is nevertheless more often than not to be understood as theory, which is never spontaneous and immediate but rather pre-thought-out and planned. This is why he states:

> Descartes could assert, and should have, the prior existence of his theory and of his pre-theoretical decision to "theorize." Or, to put it differently, theory is not born spontaneously in men but results from a previously made decision to theorize.[11]

Here Ortega criticizes Descartes for his use of theoretical or methodical doubt because it is not authentic or spontaneous. This in his estimation is not an example of prephilosophical doubt, as he considers vital-reason to be. Therefore, this manner of thinking-upon-thinking of Descartes' cogito he calls total, real, and operative *(ejecutivo)* doubt. We can sum up his notion of authenticity, therefore, in three steps:

1) First, in order for man to doubt and theorize, he must already exist in the manner of being-already-there. Man's being is always initially defined in its rootedness in the external circumstance as the real, and not in the self-as-circumstance.

2) Then, this prior and external existence both makes possible and motivates his doubt. This doubt is true, primary, radical existence, the fundamental and vital reality of living and not of doubting or thinking as a secondary act.

3) And last, man's immediate existence, prior to his theorizing, is seen as real existence, but only in retrospect. Our prereflective existence finds us in the world of the circumstance, but one can become aware of this spontaneity and immediacy only through an objective distance that can be furnished only by reflective thought.[12]

Authenticity for Ortega is thus to be found in the nature of our beliefs and never in thought. Since beliefs are held in a vital manner as an aid in living, they exhibit the true nature of man. Therefore to say in (2) above that prior existence is primary existence means to say that vital life is prior to contemplative life. And when he writes in (3) that this prior life finds us in the world of the circumstance, he means that man "finds" himself having to react to the dictates of the material world and only in this respect is man "I plus my circumstance." Thus, what Ortega means by vital-reason is best understood as:

> reason, at its most authentic. This means strictly and concretely, that the intellect as pure reason alone, does not create basic concepts but is driven to them by vital necessity.[13]

While it is true that vital-reason is authentic as immediate reality, I believe that the only way possible to arrive at any conscious recognition that "I am I and my circumstances" is through a reflective operation that confronts us with our "I" as an existent that is separate from external reality. This in essence can be construed as an example of Socratic irony.

In this respect, Ortega must be seen as a realist insofar as he makes man adapt and conform to his circumstance, where such adaptation and conformity is the authentic calling of man. This is the initial phase (thesis) of his dialectic of lived-experience. But in the process of adaptation, one also begins to question and therefore reflect on the circumstance (antithesis). The Socratic irony of which I speak is the realization that life is authentic as vitally immediate, but this can be understood only through reasoning. This reason that removes man from his immediacy also enables man to understand himself as spontaneous (synthesis). The question remains: To what degree can man continue to evolve if he ignores reason, understood in this way and follows only the dictates of vital necessity? Let us compare Ortega's thought on this topic with Sir Leonard Woolley's description of early man in his work *The Beginnings of Civilization*:

> At the beginning man, like every other animal, has been forced to adapt himself to his environment, that was the condition of his survival, and such species as failed to fulfill that condition died out. But alone of the animals man in time adopted a different solution to the problem of existence, that of adapting his environment to himself; by the control of fire, by the use of shelters and clothing, by the use of tools fabricated by himself, he could to some extent disregard the changes of climate, and instead of having to live where food abounded he made it abound where he lived.[14]

Like Woolley, Ortega also views man as being capable of adapting to the environment. But in both instances it is difficult to imagine the vital necessity that brought about the need for mathematics, classical art, or astronomy. These are not creations as are clothing, fire, and farming, which have their origins in sheer vital necessity. Ortega has argued that mathematics, for instance, is an imaginary creation that helps man understand reality.

But why does man, who is supposedly solely concerned with survival, become interested at all in explaining anything at all, much less the nature of reality, which already requires a degree of contemplative detachment from the material world? All theories, Ortega would emphasize, are inauthentic examples of a synthetic life. But where does man find the necessary impetus to afford the time and energy to even become a theoretical entity? In fact, it is difficult based on Ortega's view to understand how ideas are "things" that the mind makes up to help explain primary reality. He concedes as much:

> It is an enigma posed to our existence. To live is to be ir-revocably immersed in the enigmatic. Man reacts to this primordial, pre-intellectual enigma by activating his intel-lectual faculties, above all, his imagination. He creates a mathematical world, a physical world, a religious world, a moral world, a political world, and a poetic world, which are all effectively worlds because they each have a configuration and offered a plan, an order.[15]

But can one not argue that the creation of mathematical physics and astronomy, and the like, have as their motive a completely different point of departure than just vital necessity? When Ortega argues that life is only one ingredient in the makeup of my "I" and that the circumstance is the other, isn't this already to presuppose the existence of the conscious I as a distinct entity from the circumstance? The problem lies in the fact that what Ortega views as idealism is limited to only that which takes the form of "living within the confines of the self."[16] Idealism then, he would argue, is the product of an overzealous rationalizing and not a genuine problem brought forth by the lived-experience. In the following section we will see how this view of man interrelates with a definition of the social world that also takes the form of our circumstance.

Part I The Structure of the Social World

In closely adhering to the doctrine of historical reason as the only viable and authentic manner of living, man can only be true to himself when engaged in self-conscious reflection. The things of the world, Ortega would say, are all interpretations of reality that have exercised their authority over man while man has been too immersed in the natural attitude, without ever heeding to pay attention to his thoughts. Hence, the living-out of the doctrine of historical reason takes the worldly shape of: we do not live our lives genuinely when uncritically following the rules (metaphysical interpretations) of others (society).

To live is to live self-consciously aware of oneself as living. Hence to live an authentic life is to negate the customs of the world as far as not taking anything for granted is concerned. One cannot accept the customs, rules, and dictates of the world as legitimate unless this is done consciously. Ortega's argument is that even if we accept and embrace the reality of the life-world wholeheartedly, we must be self-consciously aware of our decision. This is certainly not an easy task since it involves a considerable degree of exegesis that man as a whole may not be ready to engage in. Regardless of this, man has to act, to use the many and varied things of the world as pragmata, but if the things of the world are pseudo-things, then our dealing with them becomes inauthentic.[17]

It is important to emphasize that Ortega's understanding of the initial state of man's authenticity is the prephilosophical natural attitude of what he considers to be the reality of early man. But given man's fall from this state of authenticity to the state of self-conscious thought, Ortega thinks that man's only salvation is to reflect and not merely to accept the interpretations of the world offered by others. This proposition is best expressed as one of all or nothing. This may indeed seem like a contradiction in Ortega's thinking, but this view has a touch of moral-existential Armageddon whereby man's original state of being is lost and cannot be recuperated, and where thus a new one must be bargained for.

Like Rousseau's notion of the gentle savage who must now contend with an alien social order, Ortega's view of authenticity offers a similar analysis of the metaphysical constitution of man. The type of being that Ortega has in mind concerning the reshaping of the moral-historical state of man is a kind of stoic who confronts the world with a critical moral-metaphysical agenda of how things "ought to be." Socrates or anyone who has ever attempted to create a world order through his own contemplation best exemplifies this manner of authenticity. The problem is that this manner of vital contemplation of which Ortega speaks has can be achieved only at the personal level and not when institutionalized. This is what he has in mind when he writes:

> In solitude, man is his truth; in society, he tends to be his mere conventionality or falsification.[18]

Man's fall from his initial prephilosophical natural attitude or mode of being has removed him from his authentic manner of existing. Given this change of paradigm, man is faced with two choices. The first choice is to attempt to return to this naturally unreflective and unrational mode of being. This of course entails the undermining of reason, scientific advancement, and the awareness of oneself as inner self-consciousness. This possibility is not a viable one given that human history appears to be pregnant, in the Hegelian sense of the word, with such historical development. This possibility is tainted with a passionately romantic bias that is practically unfeasible and that is reminiscent of the age of romanticism.

The other possibility that man is faced with entails an acceptance and understanding of man's fallen state, as it were, and a further awareness that man must act self-consciously and as responsible for his life, and therefore as aware of himself as a rational entity. One might argue that what redemption from original sin is to the Christian in the acceptance of Christ, contemplative reason is to man as salvation from worldly objectification.

Nevertheless, having analyzed this aspect of his thought in this manner, there still remains the question of how literal Ortega took this original state of being to be. This is a legitimate question since we must remember that at least part of his motivation in refuting self-conscious contemplation was essential to his refutation of Descartes.

Furthermore, what Ortega views as radical reality is precisely an understanding that man is essentially alone in his circumstance as a living entity in space and time:

> And all of this—my being that I am, and this being my world, and my living in it—all these are things that happen to me and solely to me, or to me in my radical solitude.[19]

The importance that Ortega places on solitude in describing radical reality is paramount to an understanding of his overall metaphysical anthropology or what amounts to his social philosophy. When his notion of solitude is conjoined with radical reality, it is not a term that describes a physical reality. It is instead an essential description of man as a self-conscious and autonomous entity caught in the realm of material things. This condition constitutes man's loneliness. Moreover, man's authentic life is one of a constant contemplative renewal, and one of an incessant having to address the problems and consequences of one's choices of living for oneself. Once that this reality is incorporated into the overall social world, then the authentic life will be juxtaposed with the inauthentic life exhibited by what Ortega views as the mass-man (Das Man).

Socially speaking, what Ortega holds to be the inauthentic life that is led by the mass-man is not to be identified socially with class structure. The mass-man is in fact the morally decrepit man. He is a generic type that has nothing morally positive in him to set him part from the crowd. The mass-man is the polar opposite of the self-conscious awareness found in autonomous individuality.

The mass-man in fact forms the backbone of the unreflective and uncritical collectivity. In short, the mass-man is never defined as a social phenomenon, but rather as a moral-existential one. The mass-man is the torchbearer of doxa who refuses to allow for the possibility of genuine truth, knowledge, or understanding.

The division of society into mass-man and select minority is not one of social stratification as what is referred to as upper, middle, and lower classes. Ortega defines him as follows:

> For there is no doubt that the most radical division that it is possible to make of humanity is that which splits it into two classes of creatures: those who make great demands on themselves piling up difficulties and duties; and those who demand nothing special of themselves; but for whom to live is to be every moment what they already are, without imposing on themselves any effort toward perfection; mere buoys that float on the waves.[20]

The mass-man is the one who represents the collectivity and the authentic individual consciousness that are two essentially opposite modes of existence. Both manifest themselves according to their own constitution in the life of the social world. Ortega views the arrival of the mass-man on the social scene as an unavoidable and therefore predictable condition of the popular notion of referring to society as "the people," an idea that flourished during the eighteenth century with the declaration of the rights of man. While this notion remained a juridical idea for a long period, the problems of the modern world, Ortega thinks, began when this juridical idea became a psychological state of being. At that point, the declaration of the rights of man became a usage, which he characterizes as follows:

To my mind, anyone who does not realize this curious moral situation of the masses can understand nothing of what is to-day beginning to happen in the world. The sovereignty of the unqualified individual, of the human being as such, generically, has now passed from being a juridical idea or ideal to be a psychological state inherent in the average man.[21]

Therefore, Ortega attributes the birth of this new historic level to the coming of the masses. The advent of the mass-man is to a great extent a social-political phenomenon, but it is above all a change in man's metaphysical understanding of himself. This mind shift that occurs in the eighteenth century is the fact that now the mass-man, Ortega will argue, expects and demands to be free. This is the psychological state of being that Ortega attributes to the mass-man. Now the social expectations and individual manner of behavior also change, and with them also changes man's view of himself. This modern world mentality now begins to broaden each individual's horizon, making it more difficult for each individual to be morally attuned with himself and his beliefs and values. Everyone now begins to live more in terms of the social world than during any previous time in history while at the same time neglecting his individual moral responsibility and constitution. Man now begins to lose track of his own sense of vital time in an exchange for cosmic time that lies outside of him. In losing his intuitive sense of vital time, man also loses his understanding of his vital potentiality. This loss in effect brings about, Ortega argues, a demand for unrealistic and abstract (infinite) possibilities that are beyond our reach. In other words, this state of being is juxtaposed with our vital potentiality that enables us to live up to our own possibilities by not deluding ourselves with abstract notions.

This must be reduced to the concrete in order to be realized, or putting it another way, we become only a part of what it is possible for us to be.[22]

The mere notion of the individual possibility of embracing any infinite number of life possibilities opens the door to decadence. The social world after the advent of the declaration of human rights takes on a sense of arrogance that in Ortega's estimation degrades and devalues the past. For instance, the fact that man now views his life as a program of possibilities can ideally be a noble manner of living. Yet man must now know how to utilize this newly found freedom without losing himself in the circumstance. Problems arise from the very fact that, since the scope of this program of life is greater than ever before, it therefore also finds all manners of norms, life, and principles prior to it useless. The question then becomes: What does man implement now that he has refuted the principles of the past?

The possibility of this general anxiety-ridden and directionless state of being is best exemplified by the mass-man. Mass-man then manifests the vital possibility of his being through pure action. As pure action, the life of the mass-man lacks all vital purpose and therefore he simply drifts along. This mass-man's mentality Ortega attributes to three factors: 1) liberal democracy, 2) scientific experimentation as a result of the *novum organum,* and 3) industrialization. Ortega contrasts this state of being with an eighteenth-century mentality that was ruled by: 1) obligation, 2) limitation, and 3) dependence. Mass-man now finds himself both materially spoiled and existentially bored. Here Ortega supplements his argument by citing Hegel's notion that "the masses are advancing." He also recalls Comte's contention that "without some new spiritual influence, our age, which is a revolutionary age, will produce a catastrophe," and Nietzsche's vision: "I see the flood-tide of nihilism rising."[23]

Hence the structure of the social world in Ortega's estimation is not a ready-made reality by which one is obliged to a specifically determined behavior. Instead, the social world is the result of the individual modes of life exercised by man. To this degree, the abstract social order is fashioned by the advent of juridical rights and privileges while individual, authentic, and noble life continues to be ruled by the self-administered demands of obligation and self-sacrifice. We now turn to the formation of such a world by analyzing Ortega's notion of history as consisting of an autonomous act of individual will.

Part II History as Individual Lived Experience: Inter-Individuality Theory

To exist as man-as-radical-reality is to be man-the-metaphysician. Only through such a contemplative mental state can man establish his self-consciousness as a coherent entity worthy of separation and therefore distinct from a world of mere things.

Historical reason as an offshoot of individual-lived-experience is founded on the metaphysical belief that life is always individual and as such that it is always an existential task. But this task is truly nothing in particular, only the intuition and self-awareness that one must live according to one's chosen manner. The essential problem with this view lies in that to view life as a task is already to view it as not ready-made. Thus the only way for one to make one's life is to be equipped with convictions that allow one to choose and therefore discriminate all of the other forms of life that are not suitable for our personal life-plan. This is the foundation of history as the impersonal dialectic that is life. It is also why, for Ortega all changes in humanity and in the external world are changes in beliefs or convictions:

> It is man's beliefs that truly constitute his state. I have spoken of them as a repertory to indicate that the plurality of be-liefs on which an individual, a people, or an age is grounded never possesses a completely logical articulation, that is to say, does not form a system of ideas such as, for example, a philosophy constitutes or aims at constituting.[24]

The beliefs of which Ortega speaks are never intellectual or theoretical, as we have noted in previous chapters. The belief or the network of beliefs that constitute a conviction are always vital and are therefore engaged in the function of guiding one's conduct and the performance of one's life task. History, then, is the outer manifestations of an internal dialectic of beliefs and convictions.

These outer workings of the dialectic of living have traditionally been dictated, Ortega argues, by pure reason or what he views as physico-mathematical reason. Beginning with Parmenides, who sought to know that which was invariable (being), and working his way through Aristotle, who contemplated that which changes (nature) but that does not vary, man attempted to capture reality through an apparent one-to-one relationship of thought to being, culminating in positivism. Man studies the pure and seemingly declared invariability of a being that is fixed, static, and Eleatic, and creates theories to explain his findings.

What Eleaticism accomplished, in Ortega's view, is to intellectualize being. Therefore, the task that man must preoccupy himself with is precisely the mammoth task of the disintellectualization of reality. Convictions, then, as the core of the dialectic of the lived experience attempt to question the opinions prevalent both in the past as well as the present in order to give them form and thus make concrete our immediacy. This task, Ortega gives the designation "historical reason."

> He [man] goes on accumulating being—the past; he goes on making for himself a being through his dialectical series of experiments. This is a dialectic not of logical but precisely of historical reason.[25]

The failure of this mode of reason is already inherent in its method of concentrating on the principle and not on the thing itself. Philosophy, Ortega would argue, has been misled from the beginning in supposing that being: 1) is dynamic and static, and therefore attainable; and 2) that thought is capable of fashioning an objective and quantitative method of achieving this desired end.

Ortega instead opts for Heraclitus's manner of thought.

This accumulation of being that concerns Ortega amounts to an accumulation of historical interpretations concerning reality. When this accumulation is the result of unreflective impersonal knowledge, proceeding from the world at large, he deems this inauthentic. When, on the other hand, this stockpiling is a direct result of our reflection and therefore our self-awareness, it is an authentic stage of our dialectical process of life as vital-reason.

Therefore "I am my past" in the form of its having-been-my-present as immediacy. But also, I am my past in that it is an activity that aids me in forming my present. Personal history is indeed the system of my experiences, which are "linked in a single, inexorable chain."[26] Thus, what we take to be life as biographical, emotional, and experiential reality, Ortega simply views as an inevitable and ongoing dialectic that will take place regardless of our being conscious of it or not. This existential dialectic that makes up personal life is directly responsible for the movement of history that manifests itself as quantitative and universal. For instance, Michelangelo's art is contingent on his manner of vision and the subsequent manifestation of his vision. His manner of dealing with Pope Julius II's demands, for instance, is directly linked to his overall chosen vital project. Man in Ortega's estimation is therefore free by compulsion and not just through personal choice.

The vital project that is autonomous and individual human lived experience makes up the indeterminate body of universal history. This is why Ortega contends that to understand history, it is first essential to comprehend individual life as autobiography and personal narrative and therefore as task.

Ortega sees the task of German idealism as initially a noble refutation and corrective to the ancient view of placing man in nature. The problem as he sees it, is that in idealism's creation of the *Geisteswissenschaften* and thus the reestablishment of man as *geist,* the scale tipped too far in a direction that amounts to placing man "outside" of nature through such conjectures as: cogitatio, consciousness, and apperceptions. Descartes defines the self as a *res-cogitans* and not a *res-extensa,* but Ortega argues that this is a fruitless task because what essentially unites both is extension and therefore they must coexist even though their differential quality is one of degree.

A fundamental critique of Ortega to be pointed out concerning this aspect of his thought is that while attempting to unite man with his environment, that is, the material world as circumstance, he nevertheless gives primacy to the self as a nonqualifiable and hence unquantifiable phenomenon. This is why he can make a statement such as: "The body of the other is radical and real, but his 'I' is presumed."[27]

Thus, when he states that "the appearance of the other is hypothetical,[28] he still maintains that the appearance of the other as a physical entity is obviously part of my circumstance. But the other is never simply a physical entity, but rather the subject of my interpretation as are all appearances, since he is something that lacks a permanent being and therefore is constantly making himself anew.

This constant having to deal with an "uncertain" other confronts me with my solitude as certainty. To put it another way, for Ortega the social is defined as a mutual reckoning with an unfixed other. The social level of existence is made possible by our mutual reference point that is the objective world as man's universal circumstance. This common horizon that is the physical circumstance, like Kant's notion of a universally valid world *(Allgemeingultig)* creates an openness to the existence of the other as coexistence, which in turn makes possible man's sense of "we"-ness that is society. But this closeness, this affinity that exists for the other, is always first a recognition or acknowledgment of the other as an uncertain and dynamic entity, not one based on knowledge of the other comparable to the certainty that is our self-conscious I. All that one can know about the other is that he, like myself, partakes in a solitary phenomenon that is manifested to him in his capacity as the inward being that, I too, am.[29] Thus, to know the other is always only an act of approximation and estimation that makes one question to what extent the other is like oneself, since my self-directed consciousness is all that I can be certain of. This in essence is our most generic understanding of Ortega's notion of radical reality.

When the other acts toward me, I must interpret his will, which is never fully made explicit to me. Hence, according to Ortega, the other is characterized by his actions toward me that in return make me act toward him and subsequently make me have to worry about his reaction. What amounts to the reciprocity between the other and me is truly the friction of two distinct modes of becoming, thus the mutual uncertainty in the actions of both.[30]

What the scholastics refer to as the friction between the individual and the nonindividual as the indeterminate individual, Ortega simply calls the social. The social constantly forces one to make one's I implicit or explicit as the case may be. This friction between what can be referred to as the I and the anti-I (the social) keeps one from exercising his vital reason (authenticity). This is why, for Ortega, any talk about a *Volksgeist,* whether referred to as the people, society, or the collectivity, can only be indeterminate and thus inauthentic.

> The collectivity is indeed something human, but is the human without man, the human without spirit, the human without soul, the human dehumanized.[31]

The individual is always, then, the first stage of authenticity. This is why Ortega thinks that in order to understand the nature and role of laws, the law, society, people, and so on, one must first start from an understanding of man as self, but a self that partakes in a phenomenon that is radically personal and intimate.[32] It is true that inter-individual reality brings man out of his radical solitude, but it does so only through man's capacity to imagine the being of the other as that which pertains to and which by implication resembles oneself. However, the reality that is socialization is always characterized as a secondary activity since the self is always our primary reality.

The individual is indeed compelled to live in society and therefore is capable of living with others, since there are many benefits in his doing so, but everything that he accepts must either first be reflected upon or it must be self-willed if he is to exercise his freedom as an autonomous individual. A great deal has been written by Ortega commentators about his notion of man's coexistence with his circumstance, but in reality it is the individual who wins out and whose very essence Ortega attempts to preserve.

The social is merely the setting up of the table, as it were, as the arena necessary for man to question and know the universe, since man does not exist as a disembodied soul. Everything from social customs to a salutation to a handshake to taking part in religious beliefs is already an example of inauthentic ways of being, in Ortega's view, since these are preestablished ways of being. He argues:

> It is through this social world or world of usages that we see the world of men and things, see the universe.[33]

From this we can see that individuality comes into its greatest tension with the social and collective realm in its dealing with social usages or social power, as Ortega refers to it. Social order is in essence a kind of peer pressure that coerces individuality out of itself and onto the acceptance of social customs or usages, which eventually become habits.[34] All ideas originate at a given point in time, but from the time that an idea or creative act is implemented as a usage, the original idea has already lost its allure and meaning. Ortega does not exalt individuality as mere refutation of the status quo, but he does emphasize that if one is to be true to oneself as well as to the principle of individuality, this status quo must either be accepted or rejected through a contemplative and therefore conscious effort. This is a fine example of what Ortega means by subjectivity.

In other words, the very same infrastructure that coerces man into partaking in the social realm also enables him to exercise his individuality. For instance, man speaks in order to externalize the immense inner world that he is. Thus speech itself is a manifestation of inner individuality. Man has a need and desire to communicate his inner self and this makes him a social and coexistent entity. This need can be fulfilled only in the social arena given that only there one encounters the other as reciprocity. Perhaps this is why the mere primitive usage of the phoneme, the symbol, or the signal are no longer useful at the social realm, since only through words that denote a commonly accepted meaning can man express his inner and hidden self.

Thus in concluding this chapter we realize that man's individuality expresses itself through a dialectic that is made up of both reflection as a vital impulse and experience as our metaphysical circumstance. What Ortega understands as vital-reason is in essence a mode of being human that is a return to an individually sound life based on reason that is rooted in experience. This atavistic task of living authentically is an anachronism vis-à-vis the structure of society in the modern world. Man is a historic being in the sense that he is faced with the task of forging a history for himself. The social is the offshoot of one's chosen task as biographical life or, as Ortega has said, a drama. A being that views himself as drama is already one operating on the self-conscious level. The task of life then is to maintain this level of vital intensity as the zenith of one's hierarchy of reality.[35]

Chapter Six

The Revolt of the Masses and the Nature of Mass Culture

When Ortega y Gasset published his seminal work *The Revolt of the Masses (La Rebelión de las Masas)* in 1930, he was addressing the decadent mores of Western man, albeit he did so through considerable reflection on the Europe of his day and age.[1] Ortega had previously addressed this same theme is his book *España Invertebrada,* which was published in 1929 and translated into English as *Invertebrate Spain* in 1974.[2] *Invertebrate Spain* serves as the catalyst for Ortega's analysis of the effect that existential mediocrity has on all societal values and institutions. In that book he took up the issue of moral and political leadership. He argued that in the early part of the twentieth century, people who had neither the necessary talent to lead nor the desire to transcend their own personal inadequacies were nevertheless leaders of Spanish society. These same existential shortcomings, Ortega emphasized, were brought to the institutions that they led. Thus, the "inversion" occurred due to a bold and reckless kind of leadership that was not qualified to lead, but which would neither take advice from those who were.

Thus, *Revolt of the Masses* is not an unprecedented turn in Ortega's thought. This masterful work is his attempt at a sociology of knowledge that seeks to find the foundations of societal, thus public, existence and how this is formed by vital-reason (for example, the notion of inherently lived-values in our actions). Vital reason is a central thread in the fabric of Ortega's work because it is a description of the reflective and thus subjective component of human existence. Ortega argues that every person has the responsibility of deciphering for himself the values that we embrace. From such values radiate all of our moral and thus societal actions. But, even though Ortega treats the problem of mass society in historical terms, the book nonetheless is an insightful metaphysical journey that sheds much needed understanding into the nature of man. Ortega's analysis demonstrates his acute ability for penetrating to the core of human existential concerns without recoiling into the trite and often fashionable dictates of ideology. As such, this book is an essential tool in the hands of anyone interested in what is deemed today as political philosophy. Ortega is quick to point out that all political, in fact, all social activity always recoils back into metaphysics. His collected work exhibits a well balanced and metaphysically reasoned account of reality that is often absent from other thinkers when dealing with political philosophy. And it is precisely for this very reason that this book serves as an interesting anomaly to all political catchphrases of the twentieth century, both in his day as well as today, in that it juxtaposes words like mass, minority, rebellion, and social power with currently unpopular yet classical ideas such as nobility of spirit, meritocracy, duty, individuality, and character. To judge this profound and sensitive book by its theme, one would think that materialists of all denominations would be enthralled with such a work or at least with its alluring title. But that is seemingly not the case. Ortega's analysis of mass culture does not deviate from the fundamental argument that a philosophical anthropology that does not attribute primacy to the individual can never arrive at a universal and reasoned account of man.

This chapter will concentrate on the importance of the metaphysical-existential underpinnings of presocietal values in Ortega's thought. There is no denying that man is imbued with a metaphysical, hence an existential subjectivity that allows for individuality. This existential basic reality is rooted in our ability to view ourselves as conscious entities. In other words, man is capable of a vitally prescriptive self-conscious awareness. But this is precisely what Ortega means by radical reality. This act, however, is always a pre-predicative experience. This awareness cannot be separated from our ability to fashion values for ourselves as well as for society at large. This very existential condition is always temporally driven—future-oriented, let us call it. Thus, in Ortega's work this pole of human existence will be supremely tested through the inevitable conditions that are brought about by historical human agglomeration. Therefore, the matrix for his dual notions of mass-man and noble man is always founded, at the very least, in the understanding that man is an existential being who can transcend his own temporal circumstances.

But perhaps one of the reasons why *Revolt of the Masses* does not receive the attention today that the book merits is because Ortega frustrates the illusions of positivists and other materialists by debunking their sole claim to political philosophy. He achieves this with metaphysical conceptions of personhood and the perennial philosophical question "What is man?" which positivists have always been obliged to leave to the whim of overly pragmatic social engineers. But also, it seems appropriate to point out that Ortega rejects the sociological view of man that is founded on the model of the natural sciences. Ortega's thought does not begin with a study of societal institutions, which only subsequently acknowledge the role of the individual, as is the case with materialists' theories. Instead, his overriding concern is with the nature of the individual in both his splendor and his depravity. Ortega's main point of emphasis pays close attention to the contribution that the individual brings to society. This, of course, will be criticized by positivists as being nothing other than a bourgeois metaphysical supposition. But to such a claim one can counter that a personalist rendition of human existence is always a much more accurate portrayal of human life than any collectivist approach. Hence from the first page of the book the author asserts, "It is important from the start to avoid giving to the words 'rebellion,' 'masses,' and 'social power' a meaning exclusively or primarily political."[3] Ortega's attempt at creating a constructive and rational foundation for political philosophy is basis enough for Marxists and materialists to brand him a slew of names in an attempt to discredit his work. But in the philosophy of life-tradition, we know that Ortega is not alone.[4] In scholarship, as is the case in all other interpersonal human endeavors, goodwill must remain a prerequisite rule of engagement.

The import of his disclaimer in the opening pages of this classic philosophical text is to make clear that what he means by mass-man and its counterpart, noble man, is irrespective of social standing, formal education, wealth, race, or gender. His thought is always the result of a well-thought-out analysis, and not, as he views the mass mind, often believing "that it has the right to impose and to give force of law to notions born in the cafes."[5] Having asserted this, he begins his implicit assault on all of the sacred cows that are so explicitly holy to the mind of the positivist. Ortega traces the origin of the masses, first, as a simple phenomenon of agglomeration. However, his contention is that the masses have never directed the course of history, as they have after the French Revolution. He writes:

> The individuals who made up these multitudes existed, but not qua multitude. Scattered about the world in small groups, or solitary, they lived a life, to all appearances, divergent, dissociate, apart.[6]

But this reality, he argues, has shifted, and in the process a new moral paradigm has been established. The movement of the masses into the "places of relatively refined creation of human culture has meant that the place of the noble man has been relegated to that of the chorus."[7]

However, in true Ortegan fashion, he accomplishes this analysis with metaphysical reflection, and not with political ideology. In fact, Ortega writes of the masses, "The characteristic of the hour is that the commonplace mind, knowing itself to be commonplace, has the assurance to proclaim the rights of the commonplace and impose them wherever it will."[8] The mass-man, he reasons, is that character-type who does not want to demand more of himself—one who does not attempt to transcend himself in lieu of objectifying material forces and who expects the same attitude in others. The mass-man instead, continues Ortega, "crushes beneath it everything that is different, everything that is excellent, individual, qualified and select."[9] Thus, the concept of the multitude is often nothing other than the reality of quantitative agglomeration. He concedes that this reality has always been part of the human world. However, his true distress comes about as the result of the explosion of what he refers to as "the social mass."[10] It is important to recognize that Ortega's notion of the masses is not one of a strict sociological order. Instead, his rendition of mass-man is a metaphysical-existential understanding of human life from a vital, self-reflecting consciousness. He is not merely interested in how societal values are arranged. Ortega argues that society is always made up of a combination of two factors: minorities and masses. However, the notion of minority for which he argues is nothing less than that of a nobility of effort. Whereas the mass-man, as already stated, does not signify any social class whatsoever, but a slipshod spirit of "just getting by" regardless of the consequences that such an attitude may engender. The individual who possesses a noble spirit or disposition, on the other hand, attempts to transcend his own life while simultaneously recognizing his limits. Ortega writes:

> Contrary to what is usually thought, it is the man of excellence, and not the common man who lives in essential servitude. Life has no savor for him unless he makes it consist in service to something transcendental.[11]

As I have already pointed out, this individual mass-man can be anyone. The "common man" that Ortega mentions in the aforementioned paragraph is no other than the mass-minded man. This person in question places no limits on his thought and actions when such is duly warranted. Thus, the spirit of effort never exists as the rallying point in such a life. On the contrary, concerning the nature of noble man or what he refers to as minority, Ortega has the following to say:

Hence he does not look upon the necessity of serving as servitude, as an oppression. When, by chance, such necessity is lacking, he grows restless and invents some new standard, more difficult, more exigent, with which to coerce himself. This is life lived as a discipline—the noble life. Nobility is defined by the demands it makes on us—by obligations, not by rights. Noblesse oblige. "To live as one likes is plebian; the noble man aspires to order and law" (Goethe).[12]

The philosophical cornerstone of Ortega's oeuvre is the notion that reason, in fact vital-reason as opposed to pure reason and sensualism, is central to man's knowing himself and in turn making it possible for man to engage constructively with society. Ortega's sociology runs against the current of the traditional positivist sociology, which has so often dominated that academic discipline since its inception by Auguste Comte. Ortega observes that the perennial empirical notion of social customs, environmental factors of personality, and levels of cultural differences, for instance, indeed originate and thus depend on the inherent metaphysical differences between minority (nobility) and mass-man. The noble man, then, is seen as self-imposing all three of the character-building traits so prevalent among the ancient Romans: *pietas, gravitas,* and *dignitas.* However, it is essential to point out that these two poles of human existence are not static in makeup. There exists a strain and thus a tension in human existence that allows for a free-flow transience between these poles by the same individual. Thus this notion of mass and noble man is said to cut through all traditional notions of "class." Ortega explains this phenomenon as such:

But strictly speaking, within both of these social classes, there are to be found mass and genuine minority. As we shall see, a characteristic of our times is the predominance, even in groups traditionally selective, of the mass and the vulgar. Thus, in the intellectual life, which of its essence requires and presupposes qualification, one can note the progressive triumph of the pseudo-intellectual, unqualified, unqualifiable, and, by their very mental texture, disqualified.[13]

In other words, Ortega is returning political discourse to the realm of metaphysics and also depoliticizing a portion of human reality that is not political to begin with.

Revolt of the Masses merits attention today, seventy-four years after its publication, now that conscientious people of goodwill everywhere have begun to understand the devastating results brought about by totalitarian and socially engineered societies. In this book as well as in *Phenomenology of Art, The Dehumanization of Art,* and *Man in Crisis,* Ortega manages to analyze the many guises of modernity and its lasting negative legacy on Western culture. For instance, the difference between pure science and what he refers to as technicism, he argues, is seen as a crucial impediment to the continual interest of theoretical science. Science ought to interest us, he argues, for its own intrinsic value and not as an anti-dote to applied science. About this very point he writes:

> Spengler believes that "technicism" can go on living when interest in the principles underlying culture are dead. I cannot bring myself to believe any such thing. Technicism and science are consubstantial, and science no longer exists when it ceases to interest us for itself alone, and it cannot so interest unless men continue to feel enthusiasm for the general principles of culture.[14]

Here, as throughout his collected work, the culprit is the widening axiological scope of Western societal values. The question of the spirit of science as a vital impulse that springs from a sense of wonder is given a central position in Ortega's thought. Science, he tells us, is initially a philosophical search for the unifying principles of nature, thus the ancient Greek word *physis*. But this activity demands a certain spirit in man. The scientist, Ortega argues, engages nature in a duel, as it were, where nature is challenged to come forth, to reveal its secrets. This, however, originates from an intrinsic desire for knowledge and not utility necessarily. The marriage of pure science and nineteenth-century liberalism brought about applied science, or what he refers to as technicism. Moreover, technicism, or what is referred to as technology today, is not imbued with the same quest for knowledge that is the backbone of scientific inquiry. Scientists, in becoming overly specialized, also become self satisfied and stagnated. This, too, is a form of mass-man, Ortega contends. Of this particular scientific phenomenon he writes, "He even proclaims it as a virtue that he takes no cognizance of what lies outside the narrow territory specially cultivated by himself, and gives the name 'dilettantism' to any curiosity for the general scheme of knowledge."[15] The practical applications of this technicism have immense dangers for the mass-man because these advances in science are not understood or appreciated by the masses, Ortega emphasizes. This only brings about what he calls the "psychology of the spoilt child."[16] This spoiled child as such has no self-imposed limits to his caprice and desires. These desires are perpetuated by even more demands without consideration to any sense of obligation on his part. Ortega's main argument in this regard is that the spoiled child naturally assumes that everything is always ready-made, and therefore always available on demand. The mass-man is not capable of appreciating scientific advances precisely because he does not know from where they originate. He explains:

> Thus is explained and defined the absurd state of mind revealed by these masses; they are only concerned with their own well-being, and at the same time they remain alien to the cause of that well-being. As they do not see, behind the benefits of civilization, marvels of invention and construction, which can only be maintained by great effort and foresight, they imagine that their role is limited to demanding these benefits peremptorily, as if they were natural rights.[17]

Ortega is prophetic in realizing, to the chagrin of those utopian materialist intellectuals, that the very center of all societal values, customs, social manners, economic, and political activity is first and foremost guided by an existential foundation and not by some abstract notion of material forces. Ortega's genius lies in understanding that man is what he refers to as "radical reality." This means that man must confront his own life reflectively prior to affecting any meaningful and dutiful engagement with society at large. This aspect of Ortega's philosophical work is grounded in the view that life is always presented to us first and foremost as a differentiated self. The discovery of this self allows for an existential understanding of "myself" as being something that is not merely biological. In point of fact, to hear Ortega utter his now-well-known dictum " I am I and my circumstances" is equivalent to the Socratic dictum "know thyself." Hence any collective "revolt" always goes against the core of what it means to be an individual because such an act effectively removes us from the realm of existential responsibility. Like Camus, revolt for Ortega always remains an individual and subjective reality. By addressing man as the matrix of all social-economic-political reality, Ortega makes a statement, one that makes collectivization of any kind a coerced reality in lieu of the primal freedom that pertains to the self. In this respect Ortega's thought can also be compared to that of Karl Jaspers[18] and Gabriel Marcel[19] but to name only a few twentieth-century philosophers who insist throughout their work that human life must begin in and retain wonder and awe as its key existential element. Much like Jaspers and Marcel, Ortega's disquietude over the irrationality that he viewed as damaging to philosophy and culture overall in Western culture in the twentieth century is a central theme in his work. About the little resistance and easy acceptance that he attributes to the masses regarding destructive, even though fashionable, cultural trends, he writes, "This is the new thing: the right not to be reasonable, the reason of unreason."[20] This latter reality, for instance, is one that has become entrenched in academia since Ortega's death in 1955. We have seen the outgrowth of a mindless sensualism in the likes of a dizzying array of "isms," and the proliferation of fashionable popular trends, such as deconstructionism that attempts to undermine rational objectivity and the entire history of Western philosophy. Moreover, many of these fashionable trends regard history and tradition as easy targets to dismantle, but few are imbued with the clarity and mental rigor required to seek any suitable alternative. My main criticism of the abovementioned is that most of these contemporary movements are geared toward a political situating of man, and not out of any inherent capacity or desire for knowledge proper. Ortega argues that these restless movements, anticultural collages, and manias are due to the fact that man today does everything provisionally. He writes, "Life today is the fruit of an interregnum, of an empty space between two organizations of historical rule—that which was, that which is to be. For this reason it is essentially provisional. Men do not know what institutions to serve in truth."[21] These movements can all be best summed up as being intellectual gymnastics or simply profound sounding trompe l'oeil. These trends are never concerned with a humanistic scope, but only seek to legitimize a political rendition of an apparent *bonum utile*. This of course we will frequently notice only serves to further splinter the fragile social-political virtues and values that have taken centuries to help build and nurture the open society. Thus the inherent danger in this politization of culture is that a transfer has occurred where humanistic values have been subsumed by ideology. Such themes are not alien to Ortega given that he addresses a great number of these in *Man in Crisis* (1958) and *Ideas and Beliefs* (1940). These are all examples of what Ortega viewed as mass culture.

What may often appear to some as the banal and petty concerns of intellectuals may no longer appear so trivial given a closer reading of Ortega's philosophical concerns in *Revolt of the Masses*. The reason for this is that, unfortunately, the mind of the ideologue today dictates the overall values of Western societies, whether most people realize this. Academic trends that seem naive and insipid have a way of seeping into the popular culture and filling the cultural/aesthetic vacuum that it creates with mere politics. This, Ortega argues, is partly fueled as the direct result of the narrow limits that overspecialization sets on itself. This lowering of standards is the greatest menace to Western societies, which are increasingly becoming ever more complex. This "dumbing down effect" is the result of what Ortega views as becoming used to decadence in all its manifestations. He explains, "The years are passing and there is the risk that the European will grow accustomed to the lower tone of the existence he is at present living, we will get used neither to rule others nor to rule himself. In such a case, all his virtues and higher capacities would vanish into air."[22] Ortega argues that caution ought to be observed in what are often hasty calls to change the material world in order to bring about "constructive change" in society. Change, Ortega argues, cannot be insipid or blind. That is, the ends of true reform always accommodate the demands of change for a marked improvement and do not promote the cause of an overbearing ideology. Ideology for Ortega represents the best example of the vulgarity of mass society. Ortega argues that the ideals of ideologues are bent on the destruction of institutions and not with instituting internal reform. This he views as evident in the privileged position that ideology offers to politics, which always comes at the expense of culture. This militant politization of culture is a central reason why the humanities are viewed by people in the sciences in a negative light.[23] It is important to keep in mind, as Jacques Barzun so eloquently states, that "the last thing that universities are about today is the cultivation and proliferation of culture."[24] Instead, Barzun argues, universities serve the singular function of training "professionals." Yet as current as these concerns may sound, these were all issues that Ortega addressed in his 1930 book *Misión de la Universidad (Mission of the University)*. At the very center of late-twentieth-century mass society is the self-serving quip, "But, isn't truth purely subjective, anyway?" This is an ardent example of the slipshod mentality that Ortega refers to as pertaining to the mass-man.

Hence this is what Ortega saw in the Europe of his day. At the center of culture, he tells us, always lies the essence of man. What Ortega so valiantly manages to accomplish is to bring metaphysics back into the fore of philosophy, where other popular movements of this century, such as the Vienna school along with other forms of crass materialism, have depleted it. I mention Ortega's intellectual and moral courage because he was one of the first public intellectuals who foresaw the assault on reason and especially on philosophy by positivism in its many guises as being clearly detrimental to what was once viewed as the noblest of disciplines. Today, unfortunately, the grandeur of philosophy as both a discipline of rigorous study and as a way of life, one that allows man to confront himself with what Marcel calls the "mystery of being," has been eroded. But, as we begin the twenty-first century, sensitive minds in both philosophy and science are beginning to wonder if in fact man is not truly a teleological "infinite synthesis," as Immanuel Kant has so beautifully expressed it, and not the result of mere directionless chance. If we are correct in assuming the truth of this vital belief system, we may come to the realization that all forms of "revolt" that are not anchored in a reflective self end up by simply promoting further cultural decay and moral nihilism. Ortega ends *Revolt of the Masses* with the reminder that in our epoch, some of our best attempts at reform have only managed to establish the life of the mass-man as not being representative of "a new civilization struggling with a previous one, but a mere negation."[25]

Chapter Seven

Contemplative Parallels: The Metaphysical Proximity of Valery's "Conscious Calculation" To Ortega's "Biographical Life"

Ortega y Gasset is considered throughout some philosophical circles as an existentialist, even though, as so many other existentialists, he did not welcome this description. In Spain and throughout the Spanish-speaking world, however, he is mostly seen as the leading expositor of the Escuela de Madrid (school of Madrid), a movement that includes such able thinkers as Julian Marias, Xavier Zubiri, Manuel Garcia Morente, and José Gaos. That notwithstanding, Ortega best describes his own work as ratio-vitalism or his attempt at seeking a middle ground between the gulf that has traditionally separated rationalism and empiricism. The main emphasis of his work is to situate differentiated human existence as the source of all collective and thus subsequent human endeavors. Ortega describes the subjective pole of human existence as a self-reflective activity where consciousness seeks to know itself. Thus when viewed in this historical vein, Ortega's work can also be placed alongside the Philosophy of Life movement that developed in the mid to late 1880s with the work of Wilhelm Dilthey, especially the latter's "Introduction To the Sciences of the Spirit" where he presents his cogent philosophy concerning "the idea of life" *(Philosophie des Lebens)*. Dilthey's work, whether implicitly or explicitly, has influenced the thought of thinkers such as Heidegger, Unamuno, Jaspers, Bergson, and, as already mentioned, José Ortega y Gasset. This movement, which is generally speaking centered around the notion of historical consciousness and the élan vital, is essentially a reaction against the diverse forms of Darwinism, sensualism, and positivism that dominated philosophical circles throughout most of the 1800s and the first half of the 1900s. Undeniably, these thinkers were reacting to materialism in any of its manifestations.

In this general intellectual milieu we also find some novelists, essayists, and poets. Such thinkers manage to express their philosophical reflection by means other than through philosophy per se. Among these, I want to concentrate my attention on the French poet and exemplary man of letters, Paul Valery (1871–1945). Valery's work best serves the discipline of philosophy today as a kind of fiduciary whose sole purpose is to keep academic philosophers from running aground through sheer myopia. In my estimation, the work of both of these thinkers garners the essence of philosophy in its more holistic and thus humanistic dimension. To this assertion we can add that Paul Valery was a voracious humanist. He is one of the last truly well-rounded and thus a fine example of a thinker of old, before the advent of the limiting age of specialization. Valery was intensely interested in medicine, technology, mathematics, history, philosophy, and of course literature. Furthermore, he has written extensively on all of these subjects. In terms of their respective philosophical influences, it is fair to say that both thinkers were classicists. Both Ortega and Valery had great reverence for ancient Greek and Roman philosophy and literature, especially the stoic ideal of a philosophical life. Both saw a possible reconstruction in philosophy as originating in a return to the ancients. As an example of this conviction, Ortega said that he never read contemporary journals because nothing looked less like philosophy to him than what he encountered there. Valery also did not view the philosophical work of his contemporaries with any great degree of confidence or sublimity. He writes, "If one asks oneself how philosophy nowadays would compare to traditional philosophy the answer would be that it is as a fifth-century statue compared to the featureless gods of ancient times.[1] Ortega as well saw human life in terms of a Promethean gift, which he described as a "poetic undertaking," one that is responsible for its own circumstances. A central aspect that unites these two thinkers is their belief that philosophy in the twentieth century, with perhaps the exception of existentialism, has turned its back on the question of human existence as a philosophical concern. These two thinkers use different vehicles to arrive at the same philosophical conclusion regarding meaning in human existence. Ortega's language, even though he is the philosopher of the two, is more baroque and often sensual at times. Valery, being the poet, is more laconic and analytic in his analysis. The reason for this apparent irony is that while a fine thinker in his own right, Valery attempts to surpass what he perceives as the limiting sensual world, which most poets attempt to describe. Ortega on the other hand has stated many times throughout his work that clarity is the courtesy that the philosopher owes his reader. This perhaps comes as a result of studying with such members of the school of Marburg of neo-Kantians as suchPaul Natorp and Hermann Cohen. Prior to that he had studied with Wilhelm Wundt at the University of Leipzig in 1905.

Thus, what I will attempt to demonstrate in this chapter is to showcase the work of Paul Valery, a thinker who is mainly recognized as a poet, with the work of the philosopher José Ortega y Gasset. The very essence that unites these two thinkers to each other as well as to the Philosophy of Life movement is their desire to view man, as Ortega has suggested, in terms of biographical existence as against to mere biological life. This same realization of self-conscious awareness in man Valery refers to as "a kind of conscious calculation."[2] Moreover, the most important factor that these two thinkers share in their work is their conviction that reason, that is, the intellect as an objective tool at the disposition of human life and the existential component in human existence, are not antithetical to each other. Also at issue is my contention that if a substantial reconstruction in philosophy, as both these thinkers hoped for, is ever to occur, literature in its inherent capacity to locate human existence in terms of drama or narrative can be very influential.

It is not known whether Ortega and Valery ever met or if they ever communicated. However, Ortega published a short article about Mallarme in November 1923. A month earlier he had met with another eight "friends of Mallarme" at the Madrid botanical garden to commemorate the twenty-fifth anniversary of the poet's death. The subsequent article, which came about as a result of this meeting, was published in the Spanish journal *Revista de Occidente*. Ortega concludes in this article that Mallarme's main poetical consideration is that of an exposition on the nature of silence. He refers to Mallarme's poetry as "eloquent silence." Ortega refers to such silence as being a manner of obliterating the common names of objects in order to seek their true nature. Thus, argues Ortega, all poetry helps in making the understanding of the everyday a "delicious enigma."[3] This Ortegan reverence for Mallarme's work is significant in relation to Valery precisely because today it is a well-known fact that Valery's main poetical inspiration was Mallarme.

Therefore, as a courtesy to both these thinkers as well as to the prospective reader, let us view the short list that follows, then, as a sort of linguistic propaedeutic that attempts to make clear the proper use and respective contexts in which Ortega and Valery make use of some terms that are central ingredients of their work:

1) Biographical life = an introspective and thus subjective understanding of human life that is not merely vital or biological in scope. This is equivalent to Ortega's use of "life-as-narrative" and to "life-as-drama."

2) Human existence as having-to-do *(que-hacer)* = the subjective capturing of the passage of time and how this exists in relation to human freedom.

3) Mass-man = Ortega's understanding of unreflecting and fragmented human existence. This is akin to *alteración*, or to live outside oneself. As such, this is the opposite of "noble man," or *ensimismamiento*, which is the existential condition of living within oneself.

4) "Conscious calculation" = Valery's notion of "self-conscious" awareness in man. This is the equivalent of Ortega's idea of biographical life. This is the antithesis of mass-man in the work of both of these thinkers.

5) Mind (intellect) = in Valerian terms is used more in a subjective sense than as an objective entity. By mind is meant a bridge between man the subject and, as he has said, the "chaotic" sensations that we view as the world. Ultimately mind is the essence of man, which seeks to know itself.

Among some other similar works of this same metaphysical insight and magnitude are Gabriel Marcel's *Man against Mass Society*, written in 1952, and several works by Valery including *Fluctuations on Freedom*, which appeared in 1938. Ortega's *The Revolt of the Masses* merits attention because, much like Gustave Le Bon's *The Crowd* and Oswald Spengler's *The Decline of the West*, Ortega too attempts to demonstrate that a large part of human consciousness ought to be rooted in historical consciousness. He explains:

> Hence for the first time we meet with a period, which makes tabula rasa of all classicism, which recognizes in nothing that is past any possible model or standard, and appearing as it does after so many centuries without any break in evolution yet gives the impression of a commencement, a dawn, an initiation, an infancy.[4]

In 1932, Ortega wrote a now-well-known article titled "Knowing Goethe from Within" for the German publication *Die neue Rundschau* to commemorate the centenary of Goethe's death. The significance of this article is that in it he fully explicates his idea of biographical life. Ortega asks himself: How can we know Goethe from within? How can we know anyone from within? He questions: If we ask ourselves who am I, and not just what am I, then who or what is this "I" of whom I speak throughout my existence? That "I", he replies, is not my body or even my soul, but rather my ability to know myself. He concedes that biography throughout the past, at best, has had the ability to penetrate into the psychology of people. But what he prescribes is that life be viewed as a drama or narrative where my "I" finds itself submerged in circumstances it must constantly deal with. This amounts to an existential daily renewal of our vital faculties. Human life then, he defines as I + the world (circumstances) = my life. What Ortega proclaims is a phenomenology of human life as interiority. He writes: "When something is merely an object, it is always only an aspect for another and not for itself." This is the phenomenological notion that states that while an inanimate object, for instance, exists for me as a self-conscious entity, it nevertheless does not possess existence for itself. In what amounts to a very insightful passage, Ortega likens the nature of an object to a human being when seen from outside itself. In other words, he believes that we cannot know the other from the outside. When we view our lives from within, he argues, we do not see any particular form, yet from the outside we are seen as possessing the shape or look of our bodies. He explains:

> A life looked at from its intimacy has no form. Nothing seen from inside has it. Form is always an external aspect, which a reality offers the eye when contemplated from outside, making it a mere object.[5]

Ortega believes that society is best served when all its members have encountered and thus reflected on their existence as individuals. The 1990 Nobel Prize winner Octavio Paz perhaps best exemplifies this when he writes of Ortega:

> His idea of the "I" was historical. Not the "I" of the contemplative who has shut the door on the world, but of the man in relationship—it would be more just to say, in combat—with things and with other men. The world, as he explained many times, is inseparable from the "I." The unity or nucleus of the human being is an indissoluble relationship: the "I" is time and space; or: society, history—action.[6]

The French poet/intellectual Paul Valery is a keen observer of modernity, also along the same line as Ortega y Gasset. Paul Valery was born in Cette (Sete) on France's western Mediterranean coast. Initially he studied law at Montpellier, but later opted for life as a poet. While it is true that Valery is best known as a poet, some of his better-known poems being "Le Cimetiere marin" ("The Graveyard by the Sea"), "L'Ebauche d'un serpent" ("The Outline of a Snake"), and "Au plataine" ("In the Plane Tree") it is, however, in his prose works that his true genius, if not his wisdom, is truly manifested. Valery's essays can be said to be philosophical in their overarching themes. His writing, overall, however, is that of a thoughtful and rigorous thinker. His style is clear and logical, yet not pedantic. His truly explicitly philosophical work titled *Etudes Philosophiques* is mostly geared toward the study of the mind following the methodical doubt of Descartes.

As a thinker, Valery's preoccupation with the analytic study of the mind seems rather at variance with his other poetic works of a sensual persuasion. This fascination with the life of the intellect curiously enough may be traced to the autumn of his twenty-third year. While on vacation in the Italian city of Genoa, Valery is said to have fallen in love with a woman who was a total stranger to him. This incidence of unrequited love with a Madame de Rovira has become known as the *nuit de genes,* or the Genovese night, by some biographers. This event in the young poet's life seems important in lieu of the fact that he was not to write poetry again for about the next twenty years. Instead, on his arrival in Paris in 1892, he began a twenty-year immersion in philosophy and mathematics. It is not until 1917 that Valery published another poem, the symbolic "La Jeune Parque" ("The Young Fate"). While it is very difficult and even questionable to what degree posterity can speculate on the inner workings of any thinker outside the essence of their work, I believe that Valery's negation of poetry after his disappointment with love can be compared to Descartes' drastic embracing of his methodological doubt. Descartes is the one fixed philosophical pillar on which Valery can be said to agree with. This inward turn into the nature of the self can be compared with a very early phenomenological work by Ortega y Gasset titled "Adam in Paradise" (1914), where Ortega first espouses his notion of reality as biographical life. In this work the persona that is Adam serves as a dual metaphor. In its first function, Adam is a metaphor to represent the discovery of what Ortega calls "the primordial reality of the conscious, of subjectivity" as an overarching philosophical concern. In its second function Adam serves, in effect, as the discovery of human life as biographical and existential and not merely biological, thus individual life. At this secondary level the subject begins to reflect upon itself. This concept is a major theme in Ortega's work. Similarly, Valery, in his work "Man and the Seashell," compares the creation of a seashell with the delight one feels at having what appears to be an insignificant object turn our attention on oneself philosophically. He writes:

> Among the many objects that confront man's mind with questions, some more legitimate than others, he is particularly fascinated by those, which, by their form or properties, lead him to reflect on his own powers or tendencies.[7]

Both of these thinkers are concerned with an understanding of the inner life of man. In this regard, Ortega argues that in order to be genuine, reflection must always originate within the self of its own accord. If we are to call each philosophical problem by its ascribed name, then clearly these are problems of phenomenology. But perhaps, as Heidegger best explains this, phenomenology is only a method and nothing else. Valery's work has an Ariadne's tread that attempts to establish the nature of the prereflective self. In other words, he is concerned, as Husserl and Ortega were, with what thought must be like when we are not confronting this question head-on. For instance, he writes in *Leonardo and the Philosophers,* much the same as Ortega writes throughout many of his works, that thought itself is just an element or tool at the service of human existence, however, one by which necessarily all others can be measured:

But once a philosophy has admitted or established, justified or discredited, knowledge—whether it has exalted it and developed it ultra vires by an effective combination of logic and intuition, or whether it has measured it as if it were reduced to its component parts by the science of criticism—it is invariably forced to explain—that is to express within its system, its personal system of comprehension and human activity in general, the intellectual understanding of which is, in short, only one of the modalities, although it represents the whole.[8]

Ortega points out that the problem with all notions of man when viewed as a social entity comes with the price of the neglect of the individual as he can best come to know himself. This is Ortega's impetus for arguing that man as a biological entity belongs to the collective or objective realm. However, biographical life becomes the description of the inner life of man through reflection on itself. Valery approaches this same problem by depicting the sharp subject/object distinction as a viable definition of man. The interesting thing about the work of both of these thinkers is that they both view philosophy as a search for concrete reality, not abstractions. In this respect they are both in essence saying: "What can be more concrete than my own existence?" Valery writes in regard to the nature of foresight:

To an observer watching from outside humanity, man would generally seem to act without any visible aim, as though seeing into another world, as though responding to the influence of invisible things or hidden beings. Tomorrow is a hidden potentiality. Those are some examples…foresight is the inner being, as it were, of every action which that observer I mentioned cannot understand, because he can see only what is visible.[9]

But regardless of the existentialist's approach that these two thinkers may take, their work is not to be confused with mere subjectivism. Ortega's work, for instance, is painstakingly geared toward the ratification of a midway point between idealism and realism. He achieves this with his positing that truth exists objectively for man due to the latter's anthropomorphic stance. But by the same token, he argues that man cannot exist without truth. Valery's studies on the mind, it must be pointed out, are never philosophical tracts dealing with the mind in terms of psychological analysis. Instead, his concern is always one having to do with the primacy of the mind, that is, of consciousness in relation to one's life. There is a hauntingly beautiful passage in *The Return from Holland* where he begins by describing the elation that he feels when traveling by rail. Valery links a rail journey with a narrative, which he believes effectively captures the essence of the passage of time. The work starts off by mentioning that a journey always links towns to a particular time in our lives. But he then surprises the undiscerning reader by stating that a journey can in fact be philosophical. He explains, "For me, however, the most exciting, the most philosophical thing about a journey is the interval between stops."[10] It seems remarkable today that he should be more concerned with the actual process of travel itself than with arrival at any given destination. In this context Valery juxtaposes train travel with a contemplative voyage where perhaps the final destination may turn out to be of no worldly significance, however life-affirming the discovery may be. There exists a definite correlation between this Valerian notion of travel, where the objective of locomotion is an existential buying of time, as it were, for the subject, with Ortega's very idea of politics. Whatever significance the idea of travel may have for Valery, the ultimate value that he attributes to it is never that of utility. For Ortega, too, a human existence, which is moved merely by the notion of utility, as he defines the political process, for instance, signifies the lowliest levels of the hierarchy of human values. The import of such an assertion by both thinkers, Valery in *Politics of the Mind* and Ortega in *Verdad y Perspectiva*, is that both see the contemplative life or *theoria* as higher values. This is also how Ortega came to view the study of history in *History as a System*. History for Ortega, then, can only be known by attempting to understand the time period, event, or person from their own inner constitution and not by their external appearances. That is, by seeking to know the essence that cannot readily be quantified in the historical method of recording events. This notion of the inner workings of man is perhaps best understood when Valery further writes in *The Return from Holland*:

> I see myself motionless and warmly colored behind the glass; and if I lean forward a little toward this me, a fragmentary shadow looking at me, I blot it out, annihilate myself, become one with the nocturnal chaos.[11]

Mind, according to Valery, even though not necessarily a metaphysical entity, becomes rather "a power of transformation," that is, a tool whose source and function is to combine all the other powers in nature. One of these transformations, Valery tells us, is brought about by the poet or musician when they attempt to make objective what is essentially a private inner reality. Both of these thinkers clearly view mind as creating a substantial opposition to nature. It is not that mind acts as a total negation of nature, but it does, however, separate us from our primitive state of being. The phenomenological state of prereflection best categorizes this primitive state. Ortega refutes Aristotle's notion that "all men by nature desire to know." Instead, he advocates a line of thinking more akin to Plato's, where Plato has Socrates say that we want to know precisely because we lack knowledge. This perpetually insufficient knowledge, this powerlessness in the face of a cosmic totality, serves as the impetus, Ortega argues, that attunes the tool of knowledge— the intellect—to its purpose. In short, knowledge is a need that comes about to fill a void in human existence. He explains:

> If by man's "nature" we understand, as did Aristotle, the combination of his bodily and mental endowments and

their functioning, we will have to recognize that knowledge is not "natural" to him.[12]

Valery too sees the act of knowing as an unnatural act that requires a concentrated act of will. Knowledge, he argues, is not a necessary condition to human life. In reference to this he writes "This is a non-animal condition, and wholly artificial since in fact it is not absolutely necessary to life."[13] This is a central point in Valery's work, especially in reference to his reflection on aesthetics. His contention in this respect is that nature is indifferent to individuals. As such he believes that the work of art always comes about as an opposition to life via mind. The process of human creation is always that of mental conceptualizing via perception as opposed to mere passive optical seeing. The work of the artist, according to him, is to make others create. Ironically, this is achieved because the inner workings of people cannot be communicated wholly through the work of art. Therefore, an approximation to one's inner world is the best that art can achieve. This he calls the aesthetic infinite. The work of art, then, creates a sort of aesthetic dialectic where thesis-antithesis and synthesis is perpetually reinvigorated by sensibility, which "abhors a vacuum." Valery explains:

> Here we capture the production of a work of art in its very germ. We recognize a work of art by the fact that no "idea" it can arouse in us, no act it suggests to us, can exhaust or put an end to it: However long we may breathe of a flower that accords with our sense of smell, we are never surfeited, for the enjoyment of the perfume revives our need for it; and there is no memory, no thoughts, no action that can annul its effect wholly free us from its power. That is what the man who sets out to make a work of art is striving for.[14]

This conceptualizing, which the work of art enacts, is nothing other than the power of the human mind plowing its way through sheer dislocated sensations. In *Monsieur Teste,* Valery refers to intelligence as the "power of substitution." But a substitution of what two entities? He explains that true knowledge of the world comes about through a sort of creative fidelity that organizes the diffuse impressions that we receive from our senses into coherent meaning. Valery writes:

> Intelligence is the power of substitution (as being the more adapted). Its problem would be: for any proposed group of things, or circumstances, to substitute another, such that... etc., and in this way, what was not possible becomes so. The role of language in intelligence then seems quite clear. It is a typical, fundamental substitution.[15]

The true work of the thinker, both Ortega and Valery tell us, is to unify and thus stratify the loose impressions that make up biological life. This stands true of both philosophers and poets alike. Hence, in concluding, it is important to remember the importance that Ortega attributes to silence in Mallarme's work. Truth, or what amounts to intelligible cohesion, results as an act of will in both these thinkers. Biographical life or narrative as Ortega calls it and Valery's conscious calculation in contradistinction to biological life are self-determining acts, which only a self-conscious entity can perform. In the absence of such heroic vision, man becomes, as Horace has so aptly said, a *disjecta membra* or just scattered remains.

Chapter Eight

Concluding Remarks Concerning Life-As-Radical-Reality

Part I The Existential Posture: Ortega's Philosophical Proximity To Sartre

> Hence the knowledge of the supreme unity is the goal of science and philosophy, and the healing medicine of the mind.[1]

In concluding this inquiry on the dialectical nature of the lived experience in Ortega's work, we arrive at the realization that life as task *(que-hacer)* is a derivation of life-as-radical-reality, given that the radical reality that is our natural attitude is immediate and must therefore be molded through reflection. This notion brings to fruition Ortega's idea that thought is a perennial dialogue with one's life as pertaining to both metaphysical and material circumstance. This I believe to be the case regardless of any shortcomings present in Ortega's thought. For this reason I contend that the underlying and therefore unifying theme of his work takes the form of a systematic appeal for the unity of consciousness, with its external manifestation as a biological entity. Therefore, to fully grasp the total import and implication of life-as-radical-reality, one must first understand that the purpose and goal of the statement "I am I and my circumstances." This quote serves as the genesis of an understanding that life-as-interiority must quite literally resolve itself in the "flesh."

The circumstance serves as the physical arena from where man begins to fashion his essence. However, not precluding this central theme in Ortega's thought, one gathers that there is a sense in which the world exists as an intrusion and obstacle to the fundamental essence of man-as-having-to-do. Nevertheless, such an enigmatic material intrusion is both a corrupting and necessary influence in a being that is essentially and intrinsically a subjective metaphysical entity. Indeed, we can see that, from the viewpoint of man-as-radical-reality, this intrusion necessarily occurs in a paradoxical manner. Man is an entity that can ponder its existence as being a central and unifying point from which all other subsequent realities radiate. But this necessarily also "brackets" the material world and therefore places the world in a somewhat limited state of suspended animation in order to focus upon its own inwardness as radical reality. This I say is a paradox given either of two necessary conditions: First, if there is the necessary will or vital impetus present that enables one to commit to such a perspective of personal life as introspection, then this sense of wonder itself finds the world to be an intruder. If, on the other hand, this self-referential existential commitment is missing, then any mention of such an intrusion becomes a moot point. The essential contention in this point is that life-as-radical-reality is to metaphysical concern, as is, for example, the tail of a dog that goes in endless circles trying to catch it but which discovers that there is a dog in the way. But when, on the other hand, life is not a self-referential metaphysical task, as is the case in any description of inauthenticity, then there is no tail to catch given that there is no dog in the way to pose as an obstacle.

In short, what I view as the existential posture in the fabric of Ortega's thought is what he implicitly has called life-as-radical-reality. Historical reason as a new and vital paradigm for man must consist in taking into consideration the "pulse" of the daily world as reality itself, as opposed to viewing extraordinary and recordable events as the only reality worthy of contemplation and therefore as history.[2] The reason that such a task is not readily undertaken, as Ortega would argue, is incidentally due to man's metaphysical closeness to himself. He addresses this point as follows: "Our lives are transparent to us, and what is transparent is hardest to see."[3]

Therefore, man is the result of a metaphysical union between the human being as the existent and the material circumstance (including one's body) as manifested in the world. Thus the thematic question that runs throughout Ortega's work is therefore: How does man retain or create his autonomy given that man is a reality among other entities already present in the world? I have attempted to demonstrate that this can be achieved only by attributing primacy to the self, even though not necessarily shutting off the world in the process. Perhaps this dilemma is best solved if we posit man as an existential-metaphysical entity whose makeup is substantially removed from mere material entities. In other words, any mere naturalistic model of man must be refuted because in Ortega's estimation man is not just another material entity in space and time, but is rather a self-conscious existential phenomenon. To this end, Ortega's task is closely related to that of Sartre when the latter writes in "Intentionality: A Fundamental Idea of Husserl's Phenomenology," "Consciousness and the world are given simultaneously: external by nature to consciousness, the world is also by nature related to it."[4]

This existential aspect of Ortega's work is central to his task of expositing a view of man that is inherently self referential because it helps to explain why all philosophical questioning, according to him, must always begin and end with life as the fundamental phenomenon of consideration.

Thus, so far in this essay, I have attempted to show how it is that Ortega's work is in essence a unified and to a great extent a systematic portrayal of man as an internal being that must grasp a fundamental external reality or circumstance that must be reckoned with. I have explained this theme as: 1) the dialectic of the lived experience, 2) life-as-radical-reality, 3) and I am I plus my circumstance.[5]

Moreover, these aspects of the central theme, which is the struggle to retain our subjectivity when confronted with a material and thus objectifying world, take on an existential phase. Even though the repercussions of this have been made known throughout the entirety of this essay, I will now begin to treat it in isolation.

But first, returning to the above-cited passage by Sartre, we notice that Ortega not only shared the same and varied concerns found in the existentialist corpus, but he also anticipated some of the claims of Sartre, if M. H. Hull is correct in *Ortega and Contemporary Problems: Remarks for the Ortega y Gasset International Centennial Symposium*. Hull's contention is that Ortega's work is essentially the work of an existentialist thinker regardless of the fact that Ortega was not totally at ease with this description or label of his work. He explains:

> Ortega anticipated Sartre's "I am condemned to be free" by eight years when he wrote, "I am necessarily free whether I like it or not," and Sartre's "man is nothing other than that which he makes himself" by eleven years when he wrote "man must not only create himself but he must decide what he is going to be."[6]

It is essential to note in pursuing this aspect of Ortega's thought that he and Sartre had a great deal in common that is not readily pointed out by commentators of the work of both thinkers. First it is relevant to point out that both thinkers shared a common neo-Kantian schooling that subsequently both tried to adjust to and therefore make compatible with their existential notions of life and will.

Both as well were interested in the notion of Cartesian dualism and its overall influence in modern philosophy as well as the growth of the physical sciences and their impact on spiritual life. Likewise, both men were moved by their notions of consciousness, free will, and the limiting effect that the material circumstances have on the self. In essence, both were synoptic philosophers of life.

Also, as a result of the profound influence that the thought of Husserl exercised over both thinkers, there is an undeniable residue of phenomenology found in their early work. This point is particularly central to Ortega's early hopes and aspirations of using phenomenology as a tool to unify reason and life. This, Ortega concedes, even though he goes on to explain that he dropped phenomenology as soon as he took it up because it was inadequate for his task.

Yet it remains an undeniable fact that Ortega's work, beginning with "Adam in Paradise" in 1910 to *Meditations on Quixote* in 1914 to his notions of perspectivism as well as his views on art, all exhibit a strong Husserlian influence.

For instance, if Sartre has been heralded as one of the central figures of existentialism because of his concern with the inner workings of the self, it is not difficult to view Ortega as an existentialist as well in view of their similar approach to the problem of life via Husserl's phenomenology. Let us also consider for a moment Sartre's notion of the ego as not pertaining to transcendental consciousness as compared to a similar view espoused by Ortega. This similarity is found in Ortega's existential rendition of man as natureless and thus practically essenceless.

What Sartre calls the ego, Ortega refers to as nature. But furthermore, in order to understand Ortega's notion of nature, we must understand nature to be equal with essence. In fact, when Ortega states that man has no nature, he refers to man as essenceless, as an ontological vagrant uprooted in the material circumstance. The closest that he comes to defining any semblance to a given "nature" is his notion of life. Natureless man in fact has no identity and thus he is free to become whatever he desires. Man must mold himself in his own image as long as this personal image resembles the inner and therefore vital possibilities or the personal destiny that he is capable of ascertaining.

Moreover, on the one hand, in attending to these vital possibilities man forges himself in his own image. But on the other hand, to neglect these possibilities, which are never more than just crude possibilities, never ready-made modes of being, is to turn our backs on our possibilities as existential choices. Ortega discusses what Sartre views as alienation when alienation is expressed as: "Self-Alienation" = Consciousness imprisons itself in the world in order to flee from itself.

This description of alienation is relevant to Ortega's discussion of *alteración,* since both he and Sartre view the material circumstance as given simultaneously even though always existing as external to consciousness. Ortega attempts to describe this split between consciousness and the material circumstance in his early writing, especially in the metaphor of the forest in *Meditations on Quixote.*

The forest acts as the latent field of possibilities where I am free to dwell and from where I must proceed to "depart" with an acquired perspective. That is, the forest is not unlike a metaphor to explain our material circumstance. The forest like human life itself is not viewed by Ortega as a collectivity but rather as an accidental conglomeration where all the members are absolute individuals thereof even though not physically isolated. He explains:

> From any spot within its borders the forest is just a possibility; a path along which we could proceed, a spring from which a gentle murmur is brought to us in the arms of silence and which we might discover a few steps away, snatches of songs sung in the distance by birds perched on branches under which we could pass. The forest is the aggregate of possible acts of ours which, when carried out, would lose their real value. The part of the forest immediately before us is a screen, as it were, behind which the rest of it lies hidden and aloof.[7]

Meditations on Quixote is Ortega's first attempt at explaining what I have thus far referred to as being the dialectic of the lived experience. In this work he begins to develop the many different aspects—for example, perspectivism, man-as-radical-reality, and so on—of his notion of understanding human life in terms of interiority as pinned against worldly circumstances.

Furthermore, this last aspect of Ortega's thought, which I view as existentialism, is a rather implicit phase of his thought, that even though it is evidently present from his early works, nevertheless does not fully attain its full-grown momentum until his later thought. This is significant because when we continue to compare some aspects of Ortega's and Sartre's thought, we realize that Sartre's same contention of the self never being present to itself in its immediacy, but rather through the circumstance, is precisely what Ortega means by "I am I and my circumstance." Therefore, it is while partaking in this give-and-take between myself and my circumstance that I come to know myself.

This existentialist side of Ortega's thought consists primarily of an analysis that showcases man-in-the-world as an extranatural existential phenomenon. Ortega's existentialism isolates the study of man to its biographical side and as such deals primarily with man as the inner reality that enables him to formulate his notion of man-as-radical-reality, which is from where all subsequent realities emanate.[8]

This isolation culminates in man's realization and therefore understanding that he is a metaphysical entity like no other found in the material world, and thus that he is existentially alone when confronted with his circumstances. This realization through implication brings up the question concerning solipsism and perspective, to which we will now turn our attention.

Part II The Question of Solipsism and Perspective: Biographical Life as Dialectical Reality

In this section I will take up what I consider to be a central point concerning Ortega's handling of the problem and possibility of solipsism as emanating from individual perspective as a central tenet of his doctrine of radical reality. I will attempt to demonstrate that while Ortega keeps from hermetically enclosing the self in consciousness, he nonetheless, I believe, does not succeed in effectively demonstrating how the self shares a neutral coexistence with material circumstance. Consequently, any close reading of Ortega's preoccupation with the self will demonstrate that the primacy of the self takes precedence over the circumstance as a commonsense reality and that the ideal that is the neutrality of coexistence between the self and the material world is in essence never fully and consistently attained.

My contention throughout this study, then, has been to point out that the self in Ortega's body of work necessarily enjoys a privileged and therefore primary reality by virtue of its condition of being radical reality. In short, what Ortega views as "I am I and my circumstance" is in fact a practical rendition of his task of fusing together reason and life as a vital necessity for man's living-in-the-world. There is, then, a vital necessity and therefore a possible gain that emanates from our having to deal with the material world, but it is always in retrospect that such a realization is made—always after our will and desires have been frustrated. Given the choice, man would rather not deal at all with the material world, as is the case with the ascetic, stoic, or the Buddhist, for example. This desire to negate, if not to simply learn to ignore the worldly values, as for instance, is the case with Francis of Assisi, I believe points to the fact that, existentially speaking, the self does have primacy over circumstance. Furthermore, my point all along has been one having to do with an ontological primacy of the self over circumstance, and Ortega's thought seems to be limited to the temporal, I believe, in order to accommodate the spatial-temporal circumstance. But I do not believe that he succeeds in his task of surpassing idealism.

But is it enough for Ortega to view man as coexisting with the circumstance by simply asserting that man cannot be locked up in consciousness? Is it necessary that from positing man as not being locked up in consciousness, that it also follows from this that man is ontologically on neutral footing with the material world? It is essentially important to pose this question because this is Ortega's refutation of idealism. Moreover, it has been argued that Ortega's original task was that of finding a proper place or mode of being for man in the material world. From this point he proceeds to refute idealism, perhaps from his concern that his ideas as social reformer were contingent on man's coexistence with the circumstance. But I question whether it is necessary to reject idealism altogether, if one's system mainly consists of building a manner of being for man-in-the-world. It would appear that the burden of rational and thus counterintuitive proof is on the idealist's side and not on Ortega's side. But can this burden of proof be lifted? This, I believe has indeed taken place throughout history, especially in the physical sciences. For instance, we see this in Aristarchus of Somos' argument that the sun, not the earth, is the center of the solar system. This same counterintuitive sense of wonder is also seen in Eratosthenes' measuring of the diameter of the earth, thus proving its spherical shape. And once again there is Aristarchus' argument, brought back to life in 1543 by Copernicus, that the earth was not only the center of the universe, but also that, unlike Ptolemy's theory, the earth was hurtling through space at an incredible rate of speed. Yet none of the preceding examples are self-evident and commonsense propositions.

My point is that it is misleading to believe that Ortega's position can be effectively strengthened through a successful refutation of idealism, as some commentators propose. Instead, I believe that Ortega starts out as a neo-Kantian, if only through implication, having received an extensive influence of neo-Kantian thought at Marburg under Cohen and Natorp. This appears clear if we view his explication of the trees as pertaining to phenomenon while the forest constitutes the thing-in-itself very early on in *Meditation on Quixote*.

From such neo-Kantian schooling, he then moves on to fashion his philosophy of man. That is, from this early phase of idealism as a student he moves to unite reason and life.[9] Hence it would be better to see his effort to refute idealism as the beginning of that which he found to be inadequate for his project concerning the philosophy of life. For this reason, he regrets not being acquainted with Dilthey's work prior to 1929, when he began to read him, even though he first knew of Dilthey already at the turn of the century.

Ortega's interest in the work of Dilthey should be assessed in relation to his understanding of life as biographical being, which is so central to his thinking. Throughout his early writings Ortega already exhibits a special concern for the problem of human life, even though not necessarily from a political or biological perspective, for instance, but in its overall existential dimension as phenomenon.

From his early writing, Ortega becomes interested in man as a phenomenal cosmic reality.[10] But what he lacked at that instance was an effective tool to aid him in projecting what is inward biographical reality outward onto the arena that is the material world. Anything less than this projection would seem inappropriate to him as is, for example, Husserl's notion of consciousness, which Ortega saw as a prison. Hence when he writes in "Sensation, Construction, and Intuition" that "Being is sensation, knowing, its correlative act, is feeling"[11] he is not talking about being in its classical sense, since this he views as an invention and therefore invitation to idealism. Instead, what he means is that life itself is the organ of knowledge. This is why in his estimation being and knowing are mutually dependent on each other.

Ortega, then, attempts to make life fit the mold of being, except that life is dialectical in nature and therefore is never finished until death. Life becomes synonymous with perspective, given that life is always particular and therefore concrete, never universal and abstract. By placing both biological and biographical life at the mercy of external reality, Ortega avoids and in fact refutes the problem of solipsism. But there is one respect in which Ortega, like many other thinkers, embeds his thought in what can be referred to as epistemological solipsism by stating that man as radical reality determines epistemologically what can be known. This assertion is consistent with his belief that being cannot transcend knowing because without the cognitive act (knowing), being cannot be captured. In effect, both must exist as coequals, he has argued, since being is equal to life and life is the organ of knowledge.

Dilthey therefore becomes for Ortega's later work the impetus that enables him to expound upon his theory of life-as-radical-reality. Nevertheless, while Dilthey's theory of life is well suited in aiding Ortega to develop his own theory, Ortega, however, does find some fault with Dilthey's view of consciousness. For instance, when Dilthey writes:

> Everything which exists for me is subject to the most general conditions of being a fact of consciousness. Objects are only for consciousness and in consciousness.[12]

Ortega takes issue with this notion of life as being no different from that found in idealism. Incidentally, this is the passage that Ortega uses to show that he did not get his idea of life from Dilthey. The problem with this statement, he would say, is that:

> The result, therefore, is that "there is no" such thing as consciousness as a phenomenon, but that consciousness is a hypothesis, precisely the one which we inherited from Descartes.[13]

The result of this statement is that Ortega places Dilthey in the company of Husserl and Descartes as being thinkers who "believed implicitly in consciousness."[14] His concern is that they have in their own respective ways extracted man from his circumstance, which in his estimation is tantamount to substituting life for consciousness. Therefore, in closing this section, it is my belief that Ortega's antithetical view of ideas comes about as the consequence of the polarization that exists in his work between, as has been previously stated, ideas and beliefs. This polarization occurs owing to the fact that ideas pertain to theory as the result of a conscious cognitive operation while beliefs are organic, spontaneous, and therefore rooted in the immediacy of life. Ortega therefore views consciousness as the source of ideas that subsequently exhibit an antilife disposition. Life then, for Ortega, becomes limited to the equivalent of Husserl's natural attitude of consciousness. Life is to be equated with the immediate lived experience and never with ideas. Ortega's preoccupation with life is then viewed as the emergence of a fixed and firm reality that has been stripped of all objective epistemological certainty pertaining to its material circumstance and which must subsequently turn inward to know itself.

Part III Contemplation of Existence in Terms of Interiority

> Philosophy is not a demonstrating with life what truth is, but the exact opposite, a showing what truth is so that, thanks to this, man can live genuinely. Let us then have done with intemperate melodramas and philosophize gaily, as is right and proper.[15]

When José Ortega y Gasset died in his Madrid home on October 18, 1955, he was no longer revered as the young neo-Kantian philosopher who at the beginning of the twentieth century became utterly concerned with Spain's intellectual and moral fiber. Upon his return from his self-imposed exile in 1945, Ortega was no longer a popular figure in the overall picture of Spanish cultural life. This reality possibly adds more credence to the Spanish saying that "No one is a prophet in his own land." Nevertheless, he remained a much sought after lecturer and speaker in Latin America, Portugal, and especially in Germany, where, according to him, his works were more widely read and appreciated than in Spain.

The events and outcome of the last twenty years of his life are an important asset to his thought. Ortega always held that to philosophize is by necessity to become isolated, as an outcast of sorts from the same society in which one philosophizes. He understood the life of the thinker in terms of a heroic stoicism that is always diametrically opposed to popular opinion.

This stoicism is not only important from a biographical perspective, even though this aspect is a central theme of his work, but it is also important from a philosophical viewpoint since he understood the practice of reason to be in crisis in the modern world, therefore adding to the natural state of isolation of the thinker. He believed that the life of reason has historically, but more so in modern Europe, engendered resentment, distrust, and disrespect from mass popular culture. He understood reason not only to be antithetical, but also an obstacle to the vulgarity and debauchery that he saw at the core of popular society as a whole. Such an analysis of popular culture, he argued, is the cause of such resentment.

Man then, according to Ortega, is essentially metaphysically an "unsocial" being. This is not to say that he is necessarily an antisocial being, given that this takes an active disengagement from society. Unsocial has more to do with personal temperament. Nevertheless, this contemplative temperament brings about a conflict between the individual and society, which existing as a collectivity that "without proposing to do so watches over every minute of individual life."[16] A healthy balance between the thinker and mass society, Ortega has argued, can be kept only through self-discipline, introspection, and a strong will to maintain one's subjectivity.

This discipline, introspection, and perpetually strong will that the thinker must emphasize as the prevalent themes of human life are exhibited by Ortega not only through his writings but also in his manner of biographical life. Therefore, it becomes easy to see how biographical life becomes synonymous with reflective life in the case of Ortega, given that *ensimismamiento* means to turn one's thoughts, reflection, and life inward toward oneself in an attempt for auto-evaluation. This, according to Ortega, does not qualify as a self-consciousness bracketing of the material world, therefore making the self into its own object of reflection. What he has in mind is rather a model of the contemplative life following the example of the Greeks. But the fact remains that the act of *ensimismamiento* itself, without having to be entangled in Husserlian jargon, is one of taking conscious control of one's self and thus willing and directing the course of our conscious acts.

Consequently, what Ortega brings to philosophy that must be viewed as a contribution, notwithstanding any shortcomings of his thought, is this very notion of life as biographical interiority or *ensimismamiento*. His point of departure becomes, in my estimation, his greatest and most flexible philosophical tool. In other words, he maintains that philosophy is a natural, if not the only authentic calling of man—of every man. His philosophizing has as its starting point the question of man-as-radical-reality that grounds his thought in the belief that the existence of man-in-the-world is manifested as ultimate reality.

We have seen how in regard to this aspect of his thought any talk of absolute or fixed objective being is rejected. But his understanding of man as having no fixed nature is far from arbitrary. On the contrary, he has built up a systematic system of thought, even though he may not readily refer to his thought as systematic, that empowers man with the ability to use his self-conscious will as his most practical tool. What Ortega has essentially done is to view man as a cosmic phenomenon who, even though thrown into existence, is nevertheless not totally helpless. Hence it is important to point out that Ortega's thought is never fatalistic. He has placed all responsibility and all possible glory on man's ability to make rational choices and to build a rational life for himself. In this respect, Ortega's thought is consistent with the Greek stoic notion of perseverance and endurance.

From this perspective we can see that Ortega's treatment of the will, responsibility, and subsequently of ethics is based on his respect for reason as a unifying force—that is, on logos itself. For instance, it is well known that Ortega did not maintain good relations with the Jesuits in Spain. In this regard he was anticlerical. His thought is curiously enough devoid of any substantial treatment of God as one of the classical topics of consideration in the historical philosophical canon. He does, nevertheless, make his views known concerning these matters in some of the many asides that his writing employs as hints of his overall intentions. For example, he views religion and especially Christianity, which is greatly rooted in the Spanish psyche, as paradoxical on at least three counts. First, Christianity to him is paradoxical given that one's being is not existent within oneself, but rather in (and through God). The consequences of this view are totally inconsistent with his notion of willing oneself to exist on our own accounts and merits. Therefore, he concludes by asserting that Christianity as a system of beliefs is essentially antinatural. Second, there is the paradox concerning the notion of God itself in that God is never made known to reason, which Ortega views as natural to man. God is instead known only through faith and intuition, which are in his estimation unverifiable and ultimately rooted in fear of death. And last, there is what he considers to be the paradox of the incarnation and Resurrection, whereby God is forced to come down to the realm of man in order to be known.

For these very reasons he views Christianity as antinatural in that it does not view the essence of man as a natural and sufficiently autonomous reality that can sustain itself. He views Christianity as making man its dependent and whose facticity and truth pertain to some transcendence that is not natural to man and therefore beyond him.

The difficulty for Ortega lies in his notion that life is something to be understood from within and not from outside, as any preestablished system such as Christianity would have it. His concept of life as interiority is the driving force of his thought. What life as biographical reality aims at is the elimination of any crude and naturalistic formulation of the meaning and value of life. For this reason he embarked on the study of the generations given that such a study, according to him, could furnish a better understanding of any particular life or epoch than any chronological study of history. To know someone, Ortega would say, is to know them from within given that human life is always a metaphysical struggle or strife that is not always readily externalized.

This is why it was important to ask at the beginning of this inquiry whether man simply reacts to his circumstance or if he acts freely and consciously in response to the circumstance. The answer, according to Ortega, is that the latter of these two possibilities must be the case if man is to exercise his freedom and authenticity. He cites all reflective endeavors such as poetry, art, writing, heroism, moral codes, and philosophy as attempts at overcoming the pressure exerted by the circumstance on subjectivity. In this respect man is the novelist of himself. Hence for this reason he estimates that there is a very strong and pertinent correlation between one's system of belief and one's idea of reality. The unifying principle, nevertheless, is our ability to fuse our perspective with that of the other in order to create a more coherent and panoramic view of overall reality. This then, is the true meaning of coexistence with the circumstance—with the other.

But regardless of a panoramic view of reality, this same coherence that is the result of unifying individual perspective with the many demands of the material world nonetheless ends up being absorbed by consciousness as the totality of that which pertains to itself as reality. This, stated differently, would read as: Whatever external circumstances that I incorporate into my life become part of my life as my self-conscious I. Hence consciousness must discriminate in its choices of the data that occupy its attention, according to Ortega. Consciousness, it is his belief, must always focus on something at the expense of something else.[17] For this reason, it can be argued that the contemplative person is always situating himself in the circumstance and thus is consciously aware of his ability to act and the choices that he must make concerning inner life. To this respect Ortega offers a long, but clear and direct, answer:

> The more inward the psychological theme with which one deals, the greater will be the influence of detail. The need for love is one of the most inward. Probably, there is only one other theme more inward than love: that which may be called "meta-physical sentiment," or the essential, ultimate, and basic impression which we have of the universe. This acts as a foundation and support for our other activities.[18]

The key feature in this quotation is to be found in the equating of inward life with what Ortega has called metaphysical sentiment.

In other words, metaphysical sentiment means a return of wonder to everyday life. What Ortega argues for in essence throughout his work under the aegis of life-as-radical-reality is truly a philosophy of life that attempts to recapture the philosophical, but naive, mind-set of early man. His contention is that man is the only known entity in the cosmos that can question his own existence. But also man wastes this vital and spontaneous natural attitude by allowing himself to be swallowed up by the material circumstance.

Hence to possess a sense of wonder, and exercise this as a lifelong metaphysical sentiment, is the essential foundation of human life-as-radical-reality, what amounts to Ortega's equivalent of a summum bonum. This sense of wonder allows us to unite ourself with the world, since this sense of wonder cannot remain dormant and locked within the self. Ortega's greatest contribution to philosophy is his concern that the original sense of wonder, found in early man or its equivalent found operative in the child, must be catapulted and maintained in adult life. This is the reform of philosophy which he suggests in *The Modern Theme*.

The desire for knowledge, especially for self-knowledge as Socrates stated, is Ortega's foundation for his formula of "I am I and my circumstance" as radical reality. This vital desire to question one's inner sense of life naturally spills out onto the world, since the world as a fact of consciousness, as Wittgenstein[19] asserts, is our most pressing concern. This is true given that our inner life, whether we can acknowledge this in its immediacy, is part of the totality of facts that indeed make up the backbone of the world.

Therefore, we end this section with the vital reminder that life, as Ortega has reflected, is not something that is solely lived outside of oneself on the stage of the world as some event that is "put on" for the mutual entertainment of all the parties involved. If life were merely this, it would not only be an example of life at the biological level, but rather, stated in more philosophical terms, it would be an example of the mere exercising of our inauthenticity, perhaps emanating due to our fear of death. Hence it is relevant to say that for Ortega as well as for Socrates, to philosophize as well as to live is then to be self-conscious of personal mortality and therefore to prepare for such an imminent event. But the clear overall message that makes itself known throughout Ortega's work is that the existential effects that contemplation of death can have on the common man is the same heightened awareness of life that such thoughts have on the thinker. Let us remember, then, that no matter what our worldly activities may be, no warm-blooded sentient human being can live without some degree of occasional reflection and therefore inward contemplation concerning itself. Granting that this is indeed the case as a human ideal, therefore, human life can be defined as pertaining to an existential sense of wonder that continues regardless of the circumstances. Ortega adds:

> No one lives without it, although its degree of clarity varies from person to person. It encompasses our primary, decisive attitude toward all of reality, the pleasure which the world and life, hold for us. Our other feelings, thoughts and desires are activated by this primary attitude and are sustained and colored by it.[20]

Part IV Biographical Being (Metaphysical Sentiment) vs. Biological Existence (Naturalism)

In this final section, I will conclude by stressing the profound implications that Ortega's notion of man as biographical being has on the totality of his work. This view of human existence found in Ortega is diametrically opposed to any conception or model of man as simply pertaining to a crude and simple rendition of naturalism. This is in fact what he attempts to avoid, dating back to his early work.

I have emphasized throughout this work that man as radical-reality is a genuinely metaphysically subjective reality that can be grasped only through reflection and introspection. And that viewed from the outside, the self offers only an impression of itself as a being capable of transcending the immediate and objective world. I have attempted to enumerate the diverse stages that man-as-radical-reality showcases throughout its dealings and engagements with the material world. Nevertheless, as diverse as some of these stages are, according to Ortega, they are regardless unified by 'the theme of life as a vital and inner biographical phenomenon.

Biographical life, then, can be said to be an entity that is not only capable but actually moved to live as a metaphysical sentiment. Human life as seen from within, in Ortega's judgment, is to be the sole subject of philosophy. For this very reason he attributes primacy to beliefs over ideas, since beliefs are vital and spontaneous and ideas pertain more to the sphere of calculated acts of will.

Therefore, in the process of living, man realizes, as Scheler argues, that life itself becomes the focus of all substantial questioning. This focus is derived from man's realization that he has the ability to have mastery over his life as well as from the knowledge that gradually is made known to him concerning his essence. For instance, Ortega would argue that the dialectical process that is biographical life makes evident the four classes of values found in Scheler's thought:

1) Sense values
2) Life values
3) Spiritual values
4) Religious values

The only exception that Ortega would make concerns religious values, which deals with the holy and sacred. Instead for this Ortega would substitute metaphysical sentiment. In essence, the reason that Ortega found Scheler's thought so congenial to his own is best found in Scheler's concern with the effects that the material world has on man's spiritual life, which he elaborated on in his sociology of knowledge.

As with Scheler's notion of man as an entity endowed with a

holy cosmic sense, Ortega's thought as well maintains a positive philosophical rapport with Dilthey's inner and outer categories of life. In this latter respect, Ortega's thought is a culmination of the necessity or effort exerted by a biological entity to safeguard its biographical essence as the core of its existence. This dialectic can be compared as well to Dilthey's methodology of human studies whereby man first experiences life as meaningful. Only then does the question arise as to how such meaning is expressed, and, third, how this expression makes itself understood. This dialectical principle is better studied in the case of both Dilthey, and Ortega as biography, given that this is a method of autopsychological description.

Therefore, I conclude by saying that we have seen that Ortega's work, while showing different phases during his illustrious and prolific career, is nevertheless kept centered by his notion of man as the starting point of all reality and, subsequently, of all reflection. In other words, man's authentic manner of being can be only as man-as-radical-reality, and this essential reality is brought to fruition through the dialectical process that is personal lived experience. Ortega hints at this possibility by asserting that society is an unnatural phenomenon and that man finds this setup fruitful only because he lives together in society to create "something" of benefit to all, and therefore not just for the sole purpose of such a union.[21] Insofar as social union is concerned, he will assert that only the family unit possesses an a priori sense of mutual coexistence.

This dialectical character of man-as-radical-reality, I believe, is seen in Ortega's early works, but especially in *Meditations on Quixote* whereby the theme of human life is set up as *Quijotismo*, or the study of appearance and reality. This *Quijotismo* is life-as-engagement; life as a never fixed reality that is always in the process of coming-to-be.[22]

Life, then, indeed manifests itself as the greatest dialectic of all, and I believe that, for Ortega, this process can be grasped only through a solitary and stoic attitude that makes man a conscious guardian of his essence. The contemplative life inevitably takes the form of authenticity through what the Romans referred to *pieta,* which is described as a sense of purpose and inner sensitivity that builds a metaphysical fortress around our life and that allows only that which is beneficial to its metaphysical sentiment of life.

The contemplative life, then, is said to fend off the dictates of the material world by not allowing itself to be engulfed and thus objectified. The ultimate manner of achieving such a life is through self-knowledge and not as a merely blindly acting out of one's inner self on the stage of the world. The dialectical process that is the personal livedexperience sorts out what our course of life is to be, but only if we engage in self-conscious reflection.

In essence, the mere facticity of our being-in-the world alone does not strip us of our subjectivity and thus our autonomy. But being-in-the-world without a self-conscious appeal to what our essence and therefore our role as subjectivity is—this is our greatest crime. For this reason, Ortega found the essential problems of man to be fundamentally metaphysical ones and never those pertaining to the many institutions that man has hitherto set up, ranging anywhere from religion to politics.

His work carries with it a continual importance for philosophy as a discipline, but above all as regards man as a rational-radi-cal-reality that enables us to see how all of his thought is unified by this single theme. Throughout his minor works, he warns us to be wary concerning the ominous crisis of reason that he saw as the basis for the problems of Europe in the early half of the twentieth century. He made these same concerns known as well in longer essays such as *España Invertebrada* and *The Revolt of the Masses,* and in *The Modern Theme,* where he argues for a new and vital life-oriented program that makes human life the greatest of all topics for contemplation and fascination. Part of the solution to the crisis of reason, he emphasized, is to immerse reason in life and to cultivate a strong-willed sense of individuality that maintains itself in check through rational introspection. Thus the first principle of this new philosophy of life is that:

> An idea is an action taken by a man in view of a definite situation and for a definite purpose.[23]

And if an idea acquires its authentic content and meaning in the fulfilling of the active role for which it is to function in regard to a given situation—then the life based on reason as well must find its true fate.

Moreover, Ortega teaches that the fulfilled and therefore authentic life makes human life as an end in itself through the contemplation of every pulse of this dialectic. Furthermore, life must be studied as the embodiment of a vital necessity to explain the labyrinth in which it must exist. To live, then, is to seek the essence of one's life, but to do so out of a vital desire to find the substance that enables the material world to be what it is. This is the activity that the authentic life engages in and not necessarily the detached and aloof life of purereason. Ortega writes:

> Thus, for the man given to contemplation, who follows every subject through to make it yield its innermost substance, the lightness with which the worldly man's attention skips from object to object is a cause of vexation.[24]

In effect we conclude this study with a picture of José Ortega y Gasset as the universal philosopher given to the contemplation of a time-honored and respected reality known as human existence. We also find that perhaps the very reason for which Ortega's thought has been downplayed in this age of analytic and naturalistic models of human existence may, in a twist of fate, also be responsible for a future resurgence of his thought. This I believe to be the case as modern life continues to be squeezed between, on the one hand, a scientifically oppressive model of man and, on the other, an irrational zest for esoteric gibberish that more often than not does more to deflate the meaning and value of life than it does to exalt it.

Notes

Preface

1. José Ortega y Gasset, *Meditaciónes del Quijote*, ed. Julian Marias (Madrid: Catedra, Letras Hispanicas, 1984), pp. 97-106.

2. Miguel de Cervantes Saavedra, *El Ingenioso Hidalgo Don Quijote De La Mancha* (Buenos Aires: Coleccion Literaria Sopena, 1976).

3. *Plato: The Collected Dialogues,* ed. Edith Hamilton and Huntington Cairns (Princeton: Princeton University Press, 1985), pp. 920-957.

4. I am thinking of *The Meditations* of Marcus Aurelius (A.D. 161-180) and Michel Eyquem de Montaigne's (1533-92) *Essais.* Also, of the great French tradition of essay-writing that follows in the tradition started by Montaigne.

5. Emile-Auguste Chartier, *The Gods* (London: Quartet Encounters, 1988), p. 9.

6. See Octavio Paz's book *On Poets and Others*, 1990, p. 150. Octavio Paz, who knew Ortega personally, paints a very insightful picture of Ortega as well as his writing when he writes: "All his writings were an extension of the spoken word." This is a clear and penetrating understanding of Ortega's essays. Ortega's works are essays, and as essay's they are not contained by any conventions of either genres or schools of philosophy, etc. Ortega truly does write as he spoke. This makes his works much more personable and less pedantic than the work of most academic writers, for instance.

Chapter One

1. Oliver W. Holmes, *Human Reality and the Social World: Ortega's Philosophy of History* (Amherst: University of Massachusetts Press, 1975), p. 6.

2. Circumstance = *Circum-stancia,* which for Ortega denotes all the "mute" things, events, and people that surround us.

3. José Ortega y Gasset, *Meditations on Quixote,* trans. by Evelyn Rugg and

Diego Marin (New York: W. W. Norton, 1961), p. 41.

4. José Ortega y Gasset, *Phenomenology and Art*, trans. Philip W. Silver. (New York: W. W. Norton, 1975), p. 4.

5. Ibid. Ortega never felt at total ease with any of the varieties of neo-Kantian philosophy while a student at Marburg. He viewed neo-Kantian thought as overly antiseptic and thus lacking the spontaneity found in human life. p. 44.

6. Ibid., p. 48.

7. Ibid., p. 161.

8. Ibid., p. 199.

9. Ibid., *Phenomenology And Art,* p. 57.

10. Ibid.

11. Ibid.

12. José Ortega y Gasset, *Obras Completas.* vo1.7, p. 140.

13. Ibid., *What Is Philosophy?* p. 15

14. Ibid.

15. Ibid., "Adam in Paradise." vol. I, p. 478. Later, in 1915, he views the organ and function as coexisting.

16. Holmes, *Human Reality and the Social World*, p. 55.

17. Ibid., p. 24.

18. The Spanish title is *En Torno A Galileo.*

19. Ibid., p. 36.

20. José Ortega y Gasset, *The Modern Theme.* (New York: Harper & Row Publishers), p. 60.

21. It is precisely from this notion that Ortega develops his critique of physical science. For this very reason he does not think that the essence of man will ever be effectively defined or grasped by the physical sciences.

22. Natural attitude,Ortega calls *Actitud Natural,* similar to Husserl's notion of *Naturliche Einstellung,* which the external circumstances force him to be. If

so, this would destroy the vital and subjective essence of self consciousness.

23. José Ortega y Gasset, *What Is Philosophy*, trans. Mildred Adams, (New York:: W. W. Norton, 1960), p. 41.

24. The *Encyclopedia of Philosophy*. vols. 3 and 4, ed. Paul Edwards (New York: Maxmillan and the Free Press, 1967), p. 110.

Chapter Two

1. Ortega never felt totally at ease with any of the varieties of neo-Kantian Philosophies while a student at Marburg. He viewed neo-Kantian thought as somewhat antiseptic and thus lacking the spontaneity, the drama, that he found in human life. Between April and November of 1905, Ortega studied at the University of Leipzig. There, while studying with Wilhelm Wundt, he became acquainted with the work of Nietzsche, Schopenhauer, Humboldt, and Darwin.

2. See *Meditations on Quixote* (1961, p. 13-14) for an explanation of such themes as I have mentioned. This work has been rather misunderstood, Julian Marias argues in the introduction to this text. The fact that the work has not received the critical acclaim that perhaps it deserved was already a major disappointment to Ortega in 1932. The following quotation is a central testimony of Ortega's importance as a thinker. "Towards 1932, when the book had been out for eighteen years—therefore not with undue impatience—Ortega began to call attention to it modestly. In the prologue to the first edition of his work, he repeated: 'I am myself plus my circumstance,' and he commented: 'This expression, which appears in my first book and which sums up my philosophical thought…' After some precise explanations he concluded: 'Today they have discovered this truth in Germany and some of my compatriots are now realizing it; but it is an incontrovertible fact that it was first thought in Spanish towards 1914.' In April of the same year (1932), in his article *"Pidendo un Goethe desde dentro"* ("In Search of Goethe from Within"), published in the *Revista de Occidente,* Ortega referred in a note to his relations with Heidegger: 'I am indebted but little to this author' and gave a detailed account of capital discoveries made in his own *Meditations.* 'On occasion,' he wrote with restrained melancholy,

'I am surprised that not even those nearest to me have the remotest notion of what I have thought and written. Distracted by my images they have glided over my thoughts… To find in this note things like those I am putting down may, perhaps, shame a little those young people who were ignorant of them in *good faith*. If they were acting in *bad faith* the matter would not be important; the serious thing for them is to discover that they did not know it in good faith, and that, therefore, their own good faith becomes questionable for them…As I have been silent for many years, so I shall remain again for as many more, after the brief interruption of this note, which simply leads every distracted good faith toward the right track" (p. 178).

3.   José Ortega y Gasset, *What is Philosophy?* p. 177.

4.   Ibid., p. 177.

5.   Ibid.

6.   See Ortega's essay titled "Concerning the Cosmic Phenomenal Expression: Part I, Variations Concerning the Flesh," where he directly addresses the question "What is man?" ontologically.

7.   See *Meditations on Quixote* (p.41): "Man reaches his full capacity when he acquires complete consciousness of his circumstances. Through them he communicates with the universe."

8.   Ibid., p. 57.

9.   José Ortega y Gasset, *Obras Completas.* vol. 5, p. 30.

10. El Monasterio de San Lorenzo de El Escorial is today the site of one of Spain's greatest art collections. Situated 49 kilometers from Madrid, it is bordered by the Sierra de Guadarrama and the village of San Lorenzo de El Escorial. Ortega found this forest a personal oasis. Furthermore, the forest served for him as the world-at-large. It represents the totality of the universe as an objectifying force of which we only share in as subjects, through our personal self-conscious perspective. Thus the forest "is" never to be simply equated with being the spatial-temporal totality where I find myself because it is always breaking up into a series of "angles," which overlap and which my consciousness can entertain only in isolation. The forest, then, is to reality what the handful of trees in my vicinity are to my perspective. Thus any place

in which I may subsequently find myself in the forest becomes the center of the universe—the center of reality proper. The individual trees themselves are therefore the culprits of my not seeing the entire forest.

11. Victor Ouimette, *José Ortega y Gasset* (Boston: Twayne, 1982), p. 118.

12. José Ortega y Gasset, *Some Lessons in Metaphysics*, p.18.

13. This concept is at the heart of Ortega's notion of *ensimismamiento* (authenticity), which he fully develops sometime later in his work *Ideas Y Creencias (Ideas and Beliefs)*. This proves to be one of Ortega's more "systematic" and existential works. *Ideas and Beliefs* also serves to explain his ideas of subjectivity and objectivity.

14. In this instance what is meant by dialectic is the internal (prereflective) mental monologue that takes place within consciousness; thus, befitting the definition offered in Plato's Sophist 26e by the stranger who utters: "Well, thinking and discourse are the same thing, except that what we call thinking is, precisely, the inward dialogue carried on by the mind with itself without spoken sound."

15. José Ortega y Gasset, *Some Lessons in Metaphysics*, p. 20.

16. A cornerstone of Ortega's work is the principle of individuation. This is perhaps most explicit in his work *The Revolt of the Masses*. In that work Ortega offers an in-depth analysis of the social-political reality that comes as a result of authentic and inauthentic existence. These are respectively 1) noble man and 2) mass-man. See Schopenhauer *The World as Will and Representation*, (1966, p. 352): "But the case is otherwise, and a glance into the *interior of nature* is certainly granted to us, in so far as this is nothing but *our own inner being*. It is precisely here that nature, having arrived at the highest stage up to which her activity could work, is immediately found in self-consciousness by the light of knowledge."

17. José Ortega y Gasset, *Some Lessons in Metaphysics*, p. 77.

18. The difference between "to live" and "to exist" has to do with Ortega's notion of *ensimismamiento* (authenticity) and *alteracion* (inauthenticity). But for now it will suffice to say that to live is to live passively among things. To exist, on the other hand, takes on a self-conscious and thus ontological significance.

19. José Ortega y Gasset, *Meditations on Quixote*, p. 105.

20. José Ortega y Gasset, *El Tema de Nuestro Tiempo*, Collectión Austral (EspasaCalpe S.A., 1975), p. 94.

21. Ortega's use of *reparar* and *contar-con* are related to his conception of *Ideas and Creencias* (belief). Ideas always pertain to the vitality that is the subject-pole of existence. They are not intellectual luxuries, but rather life-affirming necessities that allow us to make sense of our individual and existential condition. Beliefs on the other hand connote a collective use. They are what Ortega calls *vigencias*, or social customs. The tension that exists between the two is significant in his work because, due to this oscillation, Ortega argues, there can be a personal and private world.

22. The notion of the "I" of consciousness is rather misleading at first. His well-known formula *Yo soy yo y mis circumstancias* (I am I and my circumstances) denotes not only my external circumstances, but also the self-consciousness that locates my identity as a conscious "I" within a wider circumstance. The difficult complexity of this formula is truly understood when we realize that the third component of this formula is that "life" too is something that "happens" to me. This happenstance that is life can best be understood if we view it as analogous to Schopenhauer's notion of will.

23. See *Historical Reason* and *Goethe Desde Dentro (Goethe from Within)*, two key works where Ortega attempts to establish that history is always a bio-graphical-existential enterprise. Also see *Meditations on Hunting:* "Polybius (205?-?125 B.C.) was one of the few great minds which the turbid human species has managed to produce...He is a man of things, in the principal meaning that this word (Latin, res; Greek, pragmata) had for Romans and Greeks; that is to say, that he is a man of 'affairs'. Consequently he is concerned only with what he calls 'pragmatic thought'—that is, technical thought—and he calls his way of 'writing history'. The historic fact did not interest him because of its factual nature, much less as a pretext, as it was for many of the ancient historians, to compose, while narrating it, a compact tragedy that would excite the readers' viscera. He was interested in the 'why' of the fact; his History is a clear precursory example of what I have called 'historic reason'."

Chapter Three

1. José Ortega y Gasset, "Ideas y Creencias," *Coleccion Austral* (Madrid, 1940), p. 36.

2. Ibid., p. 18.

3. In this essay, which is a history of philosophy from 1900 to 1950, Ortega stresses that it is through the genre of autobiography that the true form of historical reason is understood.

4. *"Ideas y Creencias,"* p. 24.

5. Ibid., p. 24.

6. Beliefs are a central aspect of part of our natural attitude.

7. *"Ideas y Creencias,"* p. 28

8. Ibid., p. 32.

9. Ortega's philosophy is curiously devoid of any substantial reflection on the nature and existence of God. However this notion of belief as encompassing reason sounds relatively close to what Spanish Catholics would call faith or hope in the religious sense of the word.

10. *"Ideas y Creencias,"* p. 36.

11. Ibid., p. 35.

12. Ibid., p. 32.

13. Ibid.

14. Ibid., p. 35.

15. The notion of belief that Ortega espouses can be understood as the tradi-tional understanding of beliefs as "ideas" that we have and never question. But more important for Ortega's thought, beliefs are simply employed as meaning to showcase our being in its immediacy without the intervention of self-conscious thought. Beliefs, according to Ortega, are merely a natural manner of highlighting one's mode of being.

16. *"Ideas y Creencias,"* p. 38.

17. José Ortega y Gasset, *Concord and Liberty,* trans. Helene Weyl (New York: W. W. Norton, 1964), p. 114.

18. Convictions, I refer to in Ortega's thought, are a set of guided beliefs that are our blueprints for living.

19. *"Ideas y Creencias,"* p.49.

20. *Concord and Liberty*, p. 64.

21. Edmund Husserl, *Formal and Transcendental Logic*. trans. Dorion Cairns. The Hague: Martinus Nijhoff, 1978, pp. 4-5.

22. By no means was Ortega the only Spaniard of his period who attempted to Europeanize Spain. Ramiro de Maeztu (1874-1936) argued for the Europeanization of Spain in *Hacia Otra España* in 1899.

23. *"Ideas y Creencias,"* p. 174.

24. For Ortega this takes the form of a vital impulse to live that is prereflective.

25. *Vigencia quod viget* is the term used by Ortega to describe the totality of human life in regard to social customs, beliefs, convictions and one's overall culture.

26. Rationalism, according to Ortega, is an arbitrary belief that the behavior of things is identical to that of our ideas; hence it always leads to some form of idealism.

27. Perspective is not just a particular view. A perspective is a general sense of the world, according to Ortega, that denotes a synoptic manner of living in the world.

28. José Ortega y Gasset, *Epistolario Completo Ortega—Unamuno*. Madrid: El Arquero, 1967.

29. José Ortega y Gasset, *The Modern Theme*.

30. Philip Silver, *Ortega as Phenomenologist: The Genesis of Meditations on Quixote* (New York: Columbia University Press, 1978), p. 13.

31. José Ortega y Gasset, *Collected Letters to Unamuno*. Ortega wrote some articles comparing the respective cultures and temperaments of both Mediterranean man, in which category he placed Iberian man, as contrasted with what he viewed as the "misty" character of the German thinkers.

32. José Ortega y Gasset, "Medio Siglo de Filosofía" *Revista de Occidente,* (1951), p. 20.

33. José Ortega y Gasset, *Collected letters to Unamuno.*

34. John Frederick Nims, *Western Wind.* (New York, Random House, 1983), p. 442.

35. José Ortega y Gasset, *History As A System.* W. W. Norton & Company. New York, 1941, p. 180.

36. *The Modern Theme.* Harper Books, New York, p. 88.

37. Ibid., p.88.

38. José Ortega y Gasset, *History as a System.* p. 185.

39. Ortega's early thought was more influenced by a crude biologism (Jakob von Uexkull) than is commonly known, since his thought later took an existential posture.

40. José Ortega y Gasset, *History as a System*, p. 219.

41. Ibid., p. 220.

42. John D. Barrow, *The Anthropic Cosmological Principle* (Oxford: Clarendon Press, 1986), p. viii.

43. Philip Silver, *Ortega as Phenomenologist* (New York: Columbia University Press, 1978), p. 50.

44. Harold Raley, *José Ortega y Gasset: Philosopher of European Unity* (University, AL: University of Alabama Press, 1991), p. 197.

45. *History as a System*, p. 19.

46. Barrow, *The Anthropic Cosmological Principle*, p. 32.

47. The laws of nature as we interpret them are referred to as the constants of nature=order has a cause which is planned.

48. *History as a System*, p. 19.

49. Ibid., p. 19.

50. Ideas y Creencias, p. 31.

51. *Meditations, The Modern Theme*, and *The Buenos Aires Lectures* all depict the crisis of culture and thought.

52. Frederick Copleston, *Philosophers and Philosophies*. "Ortega y Gasset and Philosophical Relativism" (London: Search Press,1980), p. 177.

53. Silver, Philip. *Ortega As Phenomenologist*, p. 93.

54. Ibid., p. 94.

55. *History as a System*, p. 245.

Chapter Four

1. Immanuel Kant, *Critique of Pure Reason*, trans. Norman Kemp Smith (New York: The Modern Library, 1958), p. 239.

2. Ibid., p. 240.

3. José Ortega y Gasset, *History As a System*, Translated by Helen Weyl. (W. W. Norton. New York). p. 113.

4. Authenticity is *Autenticidad* in Spanish which is translated from the German *Eigentlichkeit.* p. 89.

5. Phenomenon here is to be taken in the sense of the Greek *Phainomenon* as that which reveals itself, p. 90.

6. *History as a System*, p. 116.

7. José Ortega y Gasset, *Man and People*, trans. Williard R. Trask New York: W. W. Norton, 1957), p. 16.

8. Ibid., p. 22.

9. Ibid., p. 23.

10. Ibid.

11. Ibid., p. 24.

12. Ibid.

13. Ibid.

14. Ibid., p. 28. While it remains true that writing as an impetus of early civilization ended prehistoric times, nevertheless it is relevant to note that man's earliest ancestors, the Australopithecines (which evolved into *Homo Habilis,* better known as skillful man), or what is known as the Southern Ape

about 5 million years ago already performed what are considered genuinely human activities. Such activities are described by archaeologists as: sharing food, working together as a group, and making and using tools. It is correct to assume, as Ortega has, that thought has evolved, as is today verified by anthropology, and that the capacity for reflective thought as well as brain size have indeed increased steadily from Australopithecines to *Homo habilis, Homo erectus* (Peking Man), *Homo sapiens.*

15. Ibid., p. 38.

16. Ibid., p. 40.

17. Ibid., p. 43.

18. Ibid., p. 32.

19. Ibid., p. 40.

20. Ibid., p. 45.

21. Ibid., p. 46.

22. Ortega speaks of man as being surrounded by other people and things. He describes man as being existentially engulfed by the universe. This sensation of being engulfed by the cosmos acts as a frame that gives perspective to the solitude that is individual human life more so than would be possible, say, to exist in a vacuum.

23. José Ortega y Gasset, *Man and People,* p. 49.

24. Ibid., p. 53.

25. Ibid., p. 26.

26. Ibid., p. 67.

27. Ibid., p. 70.

Chapter Five

1. José Ortega y Gasset, *Historical Reason*, trans. Philip Silver (New York: W. W. Norton, 1984), p. 72.

2. Ibid., p. 10.

3. Ibid., p. 55.

4. Ibid., p. 25.

5. Ibid., p. 21.

6. Ibid., p. 16.

7. Ibid., p. 30.

8. Ibid., p. 56.

9. Ibid., p. 62.

10. Ibid., p. 56.

11. Ibid., p. 62.

12. Ibid., pp. 64-65.

13. Ibid., p. 66.

14. Leonard Woolley, *The Beginnings of Civilization* (New York: New American Library, 1965), p. 49.

15. José Ortega y Gasset, *Historical Reason*, p. 73.

16. Ibid., p. 84.

17. What is referred to as the things of the world are best understood when we view the world as a field laden with possibilities. "Thing" involves material things, social customs, and the dominant attitudes-toward-life exhibited in any given spatial-temporal circumstance. Therefore, a pseudo-thing is one like an opinion or rumor that, once introduced into the daily world, takes on a life of its own without any apparent resistance.

18. José Ortega y Gasset, *Historical Reason*, p. 99.

19. Ibid., p. 94.

20. José Ortega y Gasset, *The Revolt Of The Masses* (New York: W. W. Norton, 1960) p. 15.

21. Ibid., p. 23.

22. Ibid., p. 22.

23. Ibid., p. 63.

24. José Ortega y Gasset, *History As A System And Other Essays Toward A*

Philosophy of History (New York: W. W. Norton, 1940), p. 167.

25. Ibid., p. 21.

26. Ibid., p. 221.

27. Ibid., *Man And People*, p. 95.

28. Ibid., p. 97.

29. Man for Ortega is an example of an entity that is predisposed by his constitution to act as a self directed consciousness and only as such can he address the world as a subsequent reality or circumstance. Seen in this respect, it is difficult to agree with Ortega's contention of his surpassing idealism.

30. Ibid., p. 175.

31. Ortega makes use of the Spanish reflexive pronoun *se,* which names someone who is in essence "no one" when he speaks of the social.

32. José Ortega y Gasset, *Man and People,* p. 190.

33. Ibid., p. 191.

34. *Vigencias* is the word Ortega uses to denote individual and thus genuine human experiences. *Supervigencias,* on the other hand, are social and aim only at mere survival; they are human petrifactions.

35. Ortega speaks of a hierarchy of reality based on our essential understanding of truth. He uses the metaphor of a "burn", first degree, second degree, and so on, to describe his notion of truth.

Chapter Six

1. José Ortega y Gasset, *The Revolt of the Masses* (New York: W. W. Norton, 1964).

2. See Helio Carpintero's *"Ortega y su psicologia del hombre-masa"* in *Un Siglo de Ortega y Gasset,* ed. Julian Marias (Madrid: Editorial Mezquita, 1984), pp. 117-130.

3. José Ortega y Gasset, *Revolt of the Masses*, p. 1.

4. See: William Barrett's *The Truants: Adventures among the Intellectuals*

(Garden City, NY: Anchor Press/Doubleday, 1982). In this reasoned yet effusive account of the utopian mind of 1930s intellectuals, Barrett, who was editor of *Partisan Review* paints an eyewitness account of this exclusive club.

5. José Ortega y Gasset, *Revolt of the Masses*, p. 18.

6. Ibid., p. 13.

7. Ibid.

8. Ibid., p. 18.

9. Ibid.

10. Ibid., p. 13.

11. Ibid., p. 11.

12. Ibid., p. 12.

13. Ibid., p. 16.

14. Ibid., p. 14.

15. Ibid., p. 110.

16. Ibid., p. 58.

17. Ibid., p. 60.

18. Karl Jaspers, *The Great Philosophers,* trans. Edith Ehrlich and Leonard H. Ehrlich (New York: Harcourt Brace, 1993).

19. Gabriel Marcel, *Man against Mass Society,* (New York: A Gateway Edition, 1962).

20. José Ortega y Gasset, *Revolt of the Masses*, p. 73.

21. Ibid., p. 184.

22. Ibid.

23. See Michael Oakeshott "The Masses in Representative Democracy" in *The Politicization of Society* (Indianapolis: Liberty Fund, 1979), pp. 313-341.

24. Jacques Barzun, *From Dawn to Decadence: 500 Years of Western Cultural Life* (New York: HarperCollins, 2000), pp. 784-785.

25. José Ortega y Gasset, *Revolt of the Masses*, p. 25.

Chapter Seven

1. Paul Valery, *History and Politics*, trans. Denise Folliot & Jackson Mathews (New York: Pantheon Books, 1962), p. 115.

2. Ibid., 118.

3. José Ortega y Gasset. *The Dehumanization of Art and Other Essays on Art, Culture, and Literature,* trans. Helene Weyl (Princeton, NJ: Princeton University Press, 1968), p. 483.

4. Ibid., p. 36.

5. José Ortega y Gasset, *Phenomenology and Art*, trans. Philip W. Silver (New York: W. W. Norton, 1975), p. 402.

6. Octavio Paz, *On Poets and Others,* trans. Michael Schmidt (New York: Arcade Publishing, 1986), p. 142.

7. Paul Valery, *Selected Writings* (New York: A New Direction Book, 1964), p. 4.

8. Paul Valery, *Leonardo and the Philosophers,* trans. and introduction by Jackson Mathews (Princeton, NJ: Princeton University Press, 1973), p. 108.

9. Paul Valery, *Politics of the Mind.* trans. and introduction by Jackson Mathews (Princeton, NJ: Princeton University Press, 1973), p. 98.

10. Valery, Paul. *The Outlook for Intelligence,* trans. Denise Folliot and Jackson Mathews. (Princeton, NJ: Princeton University Press, 1962), p. 72.

11. Ibid., p. 74.

12. José Ortega y Gasset, *The Origin of Philosophy*, trans. Toby Talbot (New York: W. W. Norton, 1967), p. 69.

13. Paul Valery, *Selected Writings,* p. 97.

14. Paul Valery, *Aesthetics,* trans. Ralph Manheim (London: Routledge & Kegan Paul, 1964), p. 76.

15. Paul Valery, *Monsieur Teste.* trans. and introduction by Jackson Mathews (Princeton, NJ: Princeton University Press, 1973), p. 96.

Chapter Eight

1. See Spinoza's intellectual love of God.

2. What Ortega has called historical reason must not only make personal life as reality a prior consideration for contemplation over the material circumstance, but it must also make it a source of vital fascination.

3. José Ortega y Gasset, "Prologue to a History of Philosophy" in *Concord And Liberty* (New York: W. W. Norton), p. 114

4. Thomas W. Busch, *The Power of Consciousness and the Force of Circumstance in Sartre's Philosophy* (Bloomington: Indiana University Press, 1990), p. 4.

5. Life as task *(que-hacer)* carries with it a sense of positive value and meaning from the field of possibilities that is the circumstance. Therefore, the circumstance does not appear as mere dead weight upon our shoulders, even though it does constitute a burden for life that must be acted on. Man is thus not a victim of circumstance but rather a molder and incorporator of the circumstance.

6. H. M. Hull, "Ortega and Contemporary Problems: Remarks for the Ortega y Gasset International Centennial Symposium," in *Ortega Centennial,* ed. José Porrua (Madrid:1985), p. 1.

7. José Ortega y Gusset, *Meditations on Quixote.* trans. Evelyn Rugg and Diego Marin (New York: W. W. Norton, 1961), p. 60.

8. Ortega's notion of life as biographical does not just serve as a convenient metaphor to explicate his philosophy. Instead, biographical for Ortega means to know oneself from within.

9. Ortega first began to read Dilthey in 1929 and, according to him, it took him four additional years to get to know him well. This unfortunate turn of events in his estimation cost him about ten years of philosophizing.

10. "Truth and Perspective" in volume 2 of *Collected Works.*

11. See "Sensation, Construction, and Intuition," (1913).

12. *Ortega y Gasset Centennial*, p. 114.

13. José Ortega y Gasset, *The Idea of Principle in Leibnitz and the Evolution of*

Deductive Theory, trans. Mildred Adams (New York: W. W. Norton, 1971), p. 281.

14. Ibid.

15. Ibid., p. 333.

16. Victor Ouimette, *José Ortega y Gasset* (Boston: Twayne Publishers, 1982), p. 147.

17. José Ortega y Gasset, *On Love: Aspects of a Single Theme*, trans. Toby Talbot. (New York: Meridian Books, 1957), p. 49.

18. Ibid., p. 93.

19. Ludwig Wittgenstein, *Tractatus Logico-Philosophicus,* trans. D.F. Pears and B.F. McGuinness (Atlantic Highlands, NJ: Humanities Press International, 1974).

20. José Ortega y Gasset, *On Love*, p. 93.

21. José Ortega y Gasset, "España Invertebrada" *Revista de Occidente,* (1971), p. 43.

22. This notion of coming-to-be is closely tied in with Ortega's notion of the generation, the generation being a period of fifteen years. Therefore, the life of man is broken down into five stages: 1) Childhood, 2) Youth, 3) Initiation, from the ages of 35 to 45, 4) Predominance, from the ages of 45 to 60, 5) Old age.

23. José Ortega y Gasset, *Concord and Liberty* (New York: W. W. Norton 1946), p. 99.

24. José Ortega y Gasset, *On Love.* p. 51.

Glossary of Ortega's Terminology

1. *Acción;* **Action**—Ortega talks of action as meaning to live by our convictions. Action does not denote social action, but rather to take an existential stance on the direction of my life.

2. *Actitud natural;* **Natural attitude**—This is the prereflective condition of taking for granted. This is equivalent to Husserl's *Naturliche einstellung* or what is also called the natural attitude.

3. *Alteración;* **Alienation**—This is the condition that Ortega attributes to "living outside of oneself." This term refers to the existential condition whereby man is not aware of his existential freedom and possibilities. *Alteración* is the opposite of *ensimismamiento.*

4. *Circumstancia;* **Circumstance**—Circumstance means all the "mute" things, events, and people that surround us. Man always finds himself in a particular circumstance. Our bodies and life are part of our circumstance.

5. *Convicciónes;* **Convictions**—The state of being convinced; firm belief founded on evidence; the act of producing mental convictions; also a proposition that is firmly believed; a set of guided beliefs that are a blueprint for living.

6. *Co-existencia;* **Coexistence**—This word means to live with our circumstance. This means that everyone must live with the objectifying forces of the external world and how these relate to our subjectivity.

7. *Contar-con*—To rely on, be aware of, or count with.

8. *Creencias;* **Beliefs**—Beliefs are vital convictions that are taken for granted. Beliefs are not ideas, but rather a prereflective (natural attitude) manner of looking at life. Beliefs are "lived."

9. *Ensimismamiento*—"To live within oneself." This term means to be self-consciously and thus reflectively aware of our existential human condition.

10. *Generación;* **Generation**—The concept of the generations is central to Ortega's overall metaphysical sociology. He argues that the three parts of human life: 1) youth, 2) maturity, and 3) old age situate our lives within very different "worlds" even though people might be contemporaries.

11. *Ideas;* **Ideas**—This term refers to the result of a rational process of understanding. The most important difference between ideas and beliefs is that ideas, unlike beliefs, are not lived.

12. *La vida es drama;* **Life-as-drama (narrative)**—This refers to Ortega's idea that life is freedom or what amounts to the lack of any fixed essence.

13. *La vida biográfica;* **Biographical life**—This is the opposite of mere biological or zoological life; the existential or internal component of human life. This is self-conscious life that recognizes itself. Biographical life pertains solely to man as an existential entity.

14. **Mass-man**—The people (or person) who find themselves "lost" or objectified by the material world. Mass-man has to do with an inauthentic state of being where man does not care to concern himself with genuine care or effort.

15. *Meditación;* **Meditation**—A meditation is not an exhaustive treatise or academic work. Instead, Ortega uses the word meditation as in *Meditation on Quixote* to mean an exploratory essay.

16. *Metafísica;* **Metaphysics**—This, Ortega argues, is a necessary tool in man's search for ultimate reality. Ortega sees the nature of metaphysics as serving as a counterbalance to all that can be quantified. He stresses that metaphysics is essential to man, but that it is something that man must want.

17. *Minoría;* **Minority**—This term appears in *Revolt of the Masses*. It means a nobility of spirit or the desire to transcend ourselves. Ortega calls this what true nobility is about. This term is the opposite of mass-man or mediocrity.

18. *Mundo patente;* **Patent world**—The physical or material appearance of reality. This reality is apprehended by immediate, vague, and imprecise impressions.

19. *Perspectivismo;* **Perspective**—Perspective is not just a particular view. Ortega argues that cosmic reality is objective, but that man can only know this objective truth through a perspective. For this reason, all perspectives point at the idea that reality is objective. A perspective is a general sense of the world that denotes a synoptic manner of living in the world.

20. *Que-hacer*—An existential having-to-do or human existence as a constant having-to-do. This is essential to the action of building our essence.

21. *Quijotismo*—This is equivalent to the concern for an uncovering of the nature of appearance and reality. In *Meditations on Quijote* Ortega argues that Cervantes is really attempting a philosophy of appearance and reality.

22. *Racionalismo;* **Rationalism**—According to Ortega, this is an arbitrary belief that the behavior of things is identical to that of our ideas; hence, according to Ortega, it always leads to some form of idealism.

23. *Realidad radical;* **Radical reality**—This is perhaps the most important idea in Oretega's work. Radical reality is a form of subjectivism where man realizes that all other "truths" originate with the differentiated individual. Radical reality is not the most important component of reality, but it is fundamental to man's building a coherent picture of cosmic reality.

24. *Ratio-vitalismo;* **Ratio-vitalism**—This is the word that Ortega uses to cite his solution to arriving at a middle ground between idealism and realism. Ortega's work is characterized by attaining a suitable solution to this problem.

25. *Razón;* **Reason**—Ortega argues against Aristotle that all men are rational. Instead, he stresses that man is a being capable of reason.

26. *Razón historica;* **Historical reason**—This is the view that all history is first and foremost a vital reality that originates in the self. To truly understand human reality, man must first know its own history.

27. *Razón pura;* **Pure reason**—Pure reason for Ortega means nothing other than the tool used in dealing with physical-mathematical conjectures. However, he critiques this kind of enterprise as saying nothing essential or definitive about human existence.

28. *Razón vital;* **Vital reason**—Vital-reason is literally the form of reason that deals with vital human concerns. Vital-reason is a form of reason that seeks to make sense of itself. Vital-reason always works in the service of human life.

29. *Reparar*—That which has traditionally been referred to as " being self-conscious" of something.

30. *Supervigencias*—As social customs that aim only at mere survival, they are human petrifactions.

31. *Vida;* **Life**—When Ortega writes about life, he always means individual or differentiated human life. To talk about life is always equivalent to mean "my life."

32. *Vigencias*—This is the word that Ortega uses to denote individual human experience amidst the totality that is human life in regard to social customs, beliefs, convictions, and our culture.

33. *Vocación;* **Vocation**—This serves as an understanding of our "direction" in life. Vocation means a self-recognition of our life as a kind of task that must be undertaken. Vocation can also refer to our "center" or "calling."

34. *Yo;* **I, Self**—This is what we refer to when we make reference to ourselves. However, Ortega argues that man is neither his body or even his life.

35. *Yo soy yo y mis circunstancias;* **I am I and my circumstances**—This is a central component of Ortega's work. This is essentially an existential concept that speaks to man's coexistence with a set of circumstances that are original to every individual and thus differentiated. Man always finds himself in a given circumstance that must be understood and dealt with.

Bibliography

Primary Sources

Ortega y Gasset, José. *Psychological Investigations*. Trans. Jorge Garcia-Gomez. New York: W. W. Norton & Company, 1987.

———. *Historical Reason*. Trans. Philip W. Silver. New York: W. W. Norton & Company, 1984.

———. "Medio Siglo de Filosofía." *Revista de Occidente*. Madrid, 1951.

———. "Parerga." *Revista de Occidente*. Madrid, 1924, p. 118.

———. "On Triumphant Sincerity." *Revista de Occidente*. Madrid, 1924, p. 158-161.

———. *The Idea of Principle in Leibnitz and the Evolution of Deductive Theory*. Trans. Mildred Adams. New York: W. W. Norton & Company, 1971.

———. *Obras Completas*. Alianza Editorial. *Revista de Occidente*, Madrid, 1983.

———. *Meditación de la Tecnica*. Colección Austral. Espasa-Calpe, S.A. Madrid, 1965.

———. *El Espectador*, vol 2. El Arquero. *Revista de Occidente*, Madrid, 1969.

———. *The Revolt of the Masses*. W. W. Norton & Company, 1960.

———. *What Is Philosophy?* Trans. Mildred Adams. New York: W. W. Norton & Company, 1960.

———. *Phenomenology And Art*. Trans. Philip W. Silver. New York: W. W. Norton & Company, 1957.

———. *España Invertebrada*. El Arquero. *Revista de Occidente*, Barbara de Braganza, 12 Madrid.

———. *Meditaciónes del Quijote*. Ed. Julian Marias. Catedra: Letras Hispanicas, Madrid, 1984.

———. *Meditations on Quixote*. Trans. Evelyn Rugg and Diego Marin. W. W. Norton & Company, 1961.

————. *Notas*. Introduction by Julian Marias. Biblioteca Anaya. L. Braille, 4-Salamanca, 1968.

————. *Ensayos Escogidos*. Aguilar, Madrid, 1967.

————. *History as A System*. Trans. Helene Weyl. New York: W. W. Norton & Company, 1941.

————. *An Interpretation of Universal History*. Trans. Mildred Adams. New York: W. W. Norton & Company, 1973.

————. *Man and People*. Trans. Willard R. Trask. New York: W. W. Norton & Company, 1957.

————. *The Origin of Philosophy*. Trans. Toby Talbot. New York: W. W. Norton & Company, 1967.

————. *Man in Crises*. Trans. Mildred Adams. New York: W. W. Norton & Company, 1958.

————. *La Deshumanización del Arte y Otros Ensayos de Estetica*. Colección Austral. Espasa-Calpe, Espana, 1987.

————. *Some Lessons in Metaphysics*. Trans. Mildred Adams. New York: W. W. Norton & Company, 1960.

————. *En Torno a Galileo*. Editorial Porrua, S.A. Mexico, 1985.

————. *El Hombre y La Gente*. Editorial Porrua, S.A. Mexico, 1985.

————. *The Dehumanization of Art*. Princeton, N.J.: Princeton University Press, 1968.

————. *"Ideas y Creencias."* Colección Austral. Espasa-Calpe, S.A., 1976.

————. *Concord and Liberty*. Trans. Helene Weyl. New York: W. W. Norton and Company, 1964.

————. *El Tema de Nuestro Tiempo*. Colección Austral. Espasa-Calpe, S.A., 1975.

————. *On Love: Aspects of a Single Theme*. Trans. Toby Talbot. New York: Meridian Books, 1957.

————. *Epistolario Completo Ortega—Unamuno*. Madrid: El Arquero, 1987.

Secondary Sources

Abellan, José Luis. *Panorama de aa Filosofía Española Actual: Una Situación Escandalosa*. Selecciónes Austral, Madrid, 1978.

Acuna, Hernan Larrain. *La Metafísica de Ortega Y Gasset: La Genesis del Pensamiento de Ortega*. Editorial Fabril, S.A. Argentina, 1962.

Allen, Reginald. *Greek Philosophy: Thales to Aristotle*. Free Press, New York, 1985.

Anderson-Imbert, Enrique. *Spanish-American Literature: A History, 1492–1963*. 2 vols. Trans. John V. Falconieri. Wayne State University Press, Detroit, 1969.

Aranguren, José Luis. *La Etica de Ortega*. Cuadernos Taurus, Spain, 1966.

Aristotle. *On Man on the Universe*. Edited by Louise Loomis. Classics Club. Roslyn, NY, 1943.

———. *The Politics of Aristotle*. Edited by Ernest Barker. Oxford University Press, Oxford, 1974.

———. *Introduction to Aristotle*. Edited by Richard Mckeon. Modern Library, New York, 1974.

Auden, W. H. *Collected Longer Poems*. Random House, New York, 1965.

Aurelius, Marcus. *Meditations*. Classics Club. Roslyn, NY, 1945.

Bacon, Francis. *Novum Organum*. P.F. Collier & Son, New York, 1922.

Barrett, William. *Death of the Soul: From Descartes To the Computer*. Anchor Books, New York, 1986.

———. *The Illusion of Technique: A Search for Meaning in a Technological Civilization*. Anchor Press, New York, 1978.

———. *Philosophy in the Twentieth Century*. Vol. 3. Random House, New York, 1962.

———. *Irrational Man: A Study in Existential Philosophy*. Anchor Books, New York, 1958.

———. *Time of Need: Forms of Imagination in the Twentieth Century.* Harper & Row, New York, 1982.

———. *What is Existentialism?* Grove Press, New York, 1964.

———. *The Truants: Adventures among the Intellectuals.* Anchor Press, New York, 1982.

Barrow, John D. *The Anthropic Cosmological Principle.* Clarendon Press, Oxford, 1986.

Bergson, Henri. *The Creative Mind: A Study in Metaphysics.* Wisdom Library, New York, 1946.

———. *The Two Sources of Morality and Religion,* trans. R. Ashley Audra and Cloudesley Brereton. Doubleday Anchor Books, Garden City, NY, 1954.

Bien, Peter. *Nikos Kazantzakis.* Columbia University Press, New York, 1972.

Blanshard, Brand. *The Philosophy of Brand Blanshard.* Edited by Paul Arthur Schilpp. Open Court, La Salle, IL, 1980.

———. *Reason and Belief.* Yale University Press, New Haven, 1975.

Boethius, Ancius. *The Consolation of Philosophy.* Trans. V. E. Watts. Penguin Books, 1969.

Bradbury, Ray. *Fahrenheit 451.* Ballantine Books, New York, 1950.

Brentano, Franz. *On the Several Senses of Being in Aristotle.* Trans. Rolf George. University of California Press, 1975.

Breuer, Reinhard. *The Anthropic Principle: Man as the Focal Point of Nature.* Birkhauser, Basel, 1991.

Brumbaugh, Robert S. *Plato for the Modern Age.* Crowell-Collier Press, 1962.

Buber, Martin. *I and Thou.* Collier Books, New York, 1958.

Camus, Albert. *The Rebel: An Essay on Man in Revolt.* Vintage Books, New York, 1991.

———. *Resistance, Rebellion and Death.* Alfred A. Knopf, New York, 1960.

———. *The Myth of Sisyphus.* Trans. Justin O'brien. Vintage Books, New York, 1991.

Busch, Thomas W. *The Power of Consciousness and the Force of Circumstances in Sartre's Philosophy.* Indiana University Press, Bloomington, 1990.

Canto, Patricio. *El Caso Ortega y Gasset.* Ediciones Leviathan, Buenos Aires, 1975.

Carr, David. *Phenomenology and the Problem of History.* Northwestern University Press, Evanston, IL, 1974.

Cervantes Saavedra, Miguel de. *Don Quixote of La Mancha.* two volumes. Trans. John Ormsby. Thomas Y. Crowell, Boston.

Cervantes Saavedra, Miguel de. *El Ingenioso Hidalgo Don Quijote de La Mancha* (Buenos Aires: Coleccion Literaria Sopena, 1976).

Chambliss, Rollin. *Social Thought: From Hammurabi to Comte.* Dryden Press, New York, 1954.

Chandler, Richard E. *A New History of Spanish Literature.* LSU Press, Baton Rouge, 1961.

Chartier, Emile-Auguste. *The Gods.* London: Quartet Encounters, 1988.

Chesterton, G. K. *Saint Francis.* Doubleday, New York, 1990.

Copleston, Frederick. *A History of Philosophy.* Doubleday, New York, 1985.

———. *Philosophers and Philosophies.* Search-Press, London, 1980.

Davies, Paul. *The Mind of God: The Scientific Basis for a Rational World.* Simon & Schuster, New York, 1992.

———. *God and the New Physics.* Touchstone Books, New York, 1983.

Davis, Harold Eugene. *Latin American Thought: A Historical Introduction.* LSU Press, Baton Rouge, 1972.

Descartes, Rene. *Meditations On First Philosophy.* Trans. Donald A. Cress. Hackett Publishing Company, Indianapolis-Cambridge, 1979.

Dimitrova, Maria. "The Relativization of Common Sense." *Man and World: An International Philosophical Review.* Vol. 27, 1994.

Eacker, Jay N. *Problems of Philosophy and Psychology.* Nelson-Hall, Chicago, 1975.

Edman, Irwin. *Arts and the Man.* W. W. Norton, New York, 1928.

————. *Philosopher's Holiday*. Viking Press, New York, 1938.

Einstein, Albert. *Relativity*. Trans. Robert Lawson. Crown Publishers, New York, 1961.

The Empiricists: Locke, Berkeley, Hume. Trans. Richard Taylor. Anchor Books. Garden City, NY, 1974.

The Encyclopedia of Philosophy. Paul Edwards, editor-in-chief. Macmillan Publishing and Free Press, New York, 1967.

Epictetus, *The Discourse of Epictetus*. Trans. George Long. George Bell and Sons, London, 1891.

Farrington, Benjamin. *Greek Science*. Penguin Books, Baltimore, 1944.

Ferris, Timothy. *The World Treasury of Physics, Astronomy, and Mathematics*. Foreword by Clifton Fadiman. Little, Brown & Company, Boston, 1991.

Field, G. C. *The Philosophy of Plato*. Oxford University Press, London, 1956.

Foster, David. *The Philosophical Scientists*. Dorset Press, New York, 1985.

Fremantle, Anne. *The Age of Belief*. New American Library, New York, 1954.

Gamow, George. *Mr. Tompkins in Paperback*. Cambridge University Press, Cambridge, 1994.

Gibbon, Edward. *The Decline and Fall of the Roman Empire*. Penguin Books, New York, 1985.

Grima Soler, Francisco. *Hacia Ortega: El Mito del Origen del Hombre*. Editorial Universitaria, S.A. Chile, 1965.

Gross, John. *The Rise and Fall of the Man of Letters: A Study of the Idiosyncratic and the Humane in Modern Literature*. New York: Macmillan, 1969.

Guinness, Os. *A Critique of the Establishment and the Counter-Counter-Culture and a Proposal for a Third Way*. Intervarsity Press, Downers Grove, IL, 1973.

Hadzsits, George. *Lucretius and His Influence*. Longmans, Green and Co., New York, 1935.

Harris, Errol E. *Cosmos And Anthropos: A Philosophical Interpretation of the Anthropic Cosmological Principle*. Humanities Press, New Jersey, 1991.

Hayek, F. A. *The Counter-Revolution of Science: Studies on the Abuse of Reason.* Liberty Press, Indianapolis, 1952.

Hegel, G. W. F. *Hegel's Logic.* Trans. William Wallace. Clarendon Press, Oxford, 1985.

———. *Philosophy of Right.* Trans. T. M. Knox. Oxford University Press, London, 1967.

Heidegger, Martin. *Poetry, Language, Thought.* Trans. Albert Hofstadter. Harper & Row, New York, 1971.

———. *Being and Time.* Trans. John Macquarrie and Edward Robinson. HarperSan Francisco, Harper & Row, 1962.

———. *Identity and Difference.* Trans. Joan Stambaugh. Harper Torchbooks, 1969.

———. *Early Greek Thinking: The Dawn of Western Philosophy.* Trans. David Farrell Krell and Frank A. Capuzzi. HarperSan Freancisco, 1984.

———. *Existence and Being.* Trans. Werner Brock. Gateway Edition, Washington DC, 1988.

Hobbes, Thomas. *Leviathan.* Edited by C. B. Macpherson. Penguin Books, 1968.

Holmes, Oliver W. *Human Reality and the Social World: Ortega's Philosophy of History.* University of Massachusetts Press, Amherst, 1975.

Houlgate, Stephen. *Freedom, Truth, and History: An Introduction To Hegel's Philosophy.* Routledge, London, 1991.

Huescar Rodriguez, Antonio. *Con Ortega y Otros Escritos.* Taurus, Madrid, 1964.

———. "Mirada A La Metaphysica," in *Revista De Occidente*, Madrid, 1964.

Husserl, Edmund. *Cartesian Meditations: An Introduction To Phenomenology,* 7th ed. Trans. Dorion Cairns. Martinus Nijhoff Publishers, Dordrecht-Boston-Lancaster, 1988.

———. *The Crisis of European Sciences and Transcendental Phenomenology.* Trans. David Carr. Northwestern University Press, Evanston, 1970.

————. *Experience and Judgment: Investigations in a Genealogy of Logic.* Trans. James S. Churchill and Karl Ameriks. Northwestern University Press, Evanston, 1973.

————. *Formal and Transcendental Logic.* Trans. Dorion Cairns. The Hague: Martinus Nijhoff, 1978.

————. *Ideas: General Introduction To Pure Phenomenology.* Trans. W. R. Royce Gibson. Collier Books, 1962.

Jaki, Stanley L. *The Purpose of It All.* Regnery Gateway, Washington, DC, 1990.

James, William. *The Varieties of Religious Experience.* Collier Books, New York, 1961.

————. *The Writings of William James.* Edited by John J. McDermott. University of Chicago Press, Chicago, 1977.

————. *The Will to Believe* and *Human Immortality* (in one volume). Dover Books, New York, 1952.

Jasper, Karl. *The Great Philosophers. Vol. 3.* Trans. Edith Ehrlich and Leonard H. Ehrlich. Harcourt Brace, New York, 1993.

Johnson, Paul. *Enemies of Society.* Atheneum, New York, 1977.

Kant, Immanuel. *Critique of Pure Reason.* Trans. Norman Kemp Smith. Modern Library, New York, 1958.

————. *The Philosophy of Kant.* Ed. Carl J. Friedrich. The Modern Library, New York, 1949.

————. *Prolegomena to any Future Metaphysics.* Library of Liberal Arts, Indianapolis, 1984.

Kaufmann, Walter. *Existentialism from Dostoevsky to Sartre.* New American Library, New York, 1975.

Kazantzakis, Helen. *Nikos Kazantzakis: A Biography Based on His Letters.* Trans. Amy Mims. Simon & Schuster, New York, 1968.

Kazantzakis, Nikos. *Saint Francis.* Trans. P. A. Bien. Simon & Schuster, New York, 1962.

———. *Report To Greco*. Trans. Peter Bien. Simon & Schuster, New York, 1965.

———. *The Odyssey: A Moderation Sequel*. Trans. Kimon Friar. Simon & Schuster, New York, 1958.

———. *Symposium*. Trans. Theodora Vasils and Themi Vasils. Crowell Company, New York, 1974.

Kierkegaard, Soren. *Fear and Trembling*. Doubleday, New York, 1941.

———. *The Sickness unto Death*. Doubleday, New York, 1941.

Krutch, Joséph Wood. *Human Nature and the Human Condition*. Random House, New York, 1959.

Kung, Hans. *Theology for the Third Millennium: An Ecumenical View*. Trans. Peter Heinegg. Doubleday, New York, 1988.

Landgrebe, Ludwig. "The Life World and the Historicity of Human Existence." *Research in Phenomenology* 11 (1981): 111-140.

———. "Phenomenology as Transcendental Theory of History." Translated by J. Huertas-Jourda and R. Feige. *Husserl: Exposition and Appraisals,* pp. 101-113. Edited by Frederick Elliston and Peter McCormick. Notre Dame: University of Notre Dame Press, 1977.

———. "The Problem of a Transcendental Science of the A Priori of the Life-World." Trans. D. Welton. *The Phenomenology of Edmund Huseerl* (six essays), p. 176-200.

———. *Major Problems in Contemporary European Philisophy: From Dilthey to Heidegger*. Trans. Kurt F. Reinhardt. Frederick Ungar, New York, 1966.

Landmann, Michael. *Philosophical Anthropology*. Trans. David J. Parent. Westminster Press, Philadelphia, 1974.

Lea, James. *Kazantzakis: The Politics of Salvation*. University of Alabama Press, Tuscaloosa, AL, 1979.

Leibniz, Gottfried Wilhelm von. *Monadology and Other Philosophical Essays*. Trans. Paul Schrecker and Anne Martin Schrecker. Bobbs-Merrill, 1965.

Lewis, C. S. *Mere Christianity*. Collier Books, New York, 1943.

Lira, Osvaldo. *Ortega En Su Espiritu*. Editorial Universidad Catolica, Santiago, 1965.

Marias, Julian. *Generations: A Historical Method*. Trans. Harold C. Raley. University of Alabama Press, University, AL. 1967.

———. *La Escuela de Madrid: Estudios de Filosofía Española*. Biblioteca de Occidente. Emece Editores, Buenos Aires, 1959.

———. *Historia de Filosofía*. Biblioteca de la Revista de Occidente. General Mola, 11 Madrid.

Marrero, Vicente. *Ortega, Filosofo "Mondain."* Ediciónes Rialpa, S.A. Madrid, 1961.

McClintock, Robert. *Man and His Circumstances: Ortega as Educator*. Teachers College Press, Columbia University. New York, 1971.

Mill, John Stuart. *Utilitarianism: On Liberty, Considerations on Representative Government*. Everyman's Library, 1992.

Mohanty, J. N. "Life-World and A Priori in Husserl's Later Thought," in *Analecta Husseliana*. Vol. 3, pp. 46-65.

de la Mora, Fernandez Gonzalo. *Filosofos Espanoles-del Siglo XX*. Colección Ensayo, Barcelona, 1987.

Mora, Ferrater José. *Diccionario de Filosofía*. Editorial Sudamericana, Buenos Aires, 1969.

———. *Man at the Crossroads*. Beacon Press, Beacon Hill, Boston. 1954.

———. *Obras Selectas Volume I*. Ediciones de la Revista de Occidente. Barbara de Braganza, 12. Madrid, 1967.

Morillas-Lopez, Juan. *The Krausist Movement and Ideological Change in Spain, 1854-1874*. Cambridge University Press, London, 1980.

Moron, Ciriaco Arroyo. *El Sistema de Ortega y Gasset*. Ediciones Alcala, Madrid, 1968.

Morrison, James C. "Husserl's Crisis: Reflections on the Relationship of Philosophy and History." *Philosophy and Phenomenological Research* 37 (1977): 312-330. Ithaca: Cornell University Press, 1983.

Nabokov, Vladimir. *Strong Opinions*. Vintage International, New York, 1973.

Newmark, Maxim. *Dictionary of Spanish Literature*. Philosophical Library, New York, 1956.

Nietzsche, Friedrich. *Beyond Good and Evil: Prelude to a Philosophy of the Future*. Trans. Walter Kaufmann. Vintage Books, New York, 1966.

———. *The Birth of Tragedy*. Trans. Walter Kaufmann. Vintage books, New York, 1967.

———. *The Case of Wagner*. Trans. Walter Kaufmann. Vintage Books, New York, 1967.

———. *Thus Spoke Zarathustra*. Trans. Thomas Common. The Modern Library, New York.

———. *On the Genealogy of Morals*. Trans. Walter Kaufmann and R. J. Hollingdale. Random House, New York, 1966.

———. *Ecce Homo*. Trans. Walter Kaufmann. Random House, New York, 1966.

———. *The Portable Nietzsche*. Ed. and trans. Walter Kaufmann. Penguin Books, New York, 1976.

Nims, John Frederick. *Western Wind: An Introduction to Poetry*. Random House, New York, 1983.

Ortega y Gasset Centennial (Centenario Ortega y Gasset). Ediciónes José Porrua Turanza, S.A. Madrid, 1985.

Ouimette, Victor. *José Ortega y Gasset*. Twayne Publishers, Boston, 1982

Paz, Octavio. *On Poets and Others*. New York: Arcade Publishing, 1990.

Penrose, Roger. *The Emperor's New Mind: Concerning Computers, Minds, and The Laws of Physics*. Oxford University Press, Oxford, 1989.

Peters, F. E. *Greek Philosophical Terms: A Historical Lexicon*. New York University Press, New York, 1967.

Pfander, Alexander. *Phenomenology of Willing and Motivation*. Trans. Herbert Spiegelberg. Northwestern University Press, Evanston, IL, 1967.

The Philosophy of Hegel. Ed. Carl J. Friedrich. The Modern Library, New York, 1953.

Plato. *The Republic.* Trans. Francis Cornford. Oxford University Press, London, 1945.

———. *Euthyphro, Apology, Crito.* Trans. F. J. Church. Liberal Arts Library, Indianapolis, 1981.

———. *Collected Dialogues.* Ed. Edith Hamilton and Huntington Cairns. Princeton University Press, Princeton, 1985.

Pletsch, Carl. *Young Nietzsche: Becoming a Genius.* The Free Press, New York, 1991.

Plotinus, *The Six Enneads.* Trans. Stephen MacKenna and B. S. Page. Encyclopedia Britannica, Chicago, 1952.

Putnam, Hilary. *The Many Faces of Realism.* Open Court, LaSalle, IL, 1987.

Putnam, Walter. *Paul Valery Revisited.* Twayne Publishers, New York, 1995.

Raley, Harold C. *José Ortega y Gasset: Philosopher of European Unity.* University of Alabama Press, 1971.

The Rationalists: Descartes, Spinoza, Leibniz. Trans. John Veitch, R. H. M. Elwes, Albert Chandler. Anchor Books, Garden City, NY, 1974.

Riestra, Miguel A. *Fundamentos Filosoficos de la Educación.* Editorial Universitaria, Universidad de Puerto Rico, 1974.

Rodriguez, Ramon. "Las Declaraciones Postumas de Heidegger." An interview in *Der Spiegel,* 1966.

Rosen, Joe. *The Capricious Cosmos.* Macmillan Publishing, 1991 .

Santayana, George. *Skepticism and Animal Faith.* Dover Books, New York, 1955.

———. *The Sense of Beauty.* Dover Books, New York, 1955.

Sartre, Jean-Paul. *Being and Nothingness: An Essay in Phenomenological Ontology.* Trans. Hazel E. Barnes. Citadel Press, Secaucus, NJ, 1974.

———. *Existentialism and Human Emotions.* Wisdom Library, New York, 1957.

Scheler, Max. *Problems of a Sociology of Knowledge.* Trans. Manfred S. Frings. Edited by Kenneth W. Stikkers. Routledge & Kegan Paul, London, Boston, and Henley, 1980.

———. *Ressentiment.* Edited by Lewis A. Coser. Schocken Books, New York, 1961.

———. *Formalism in Ethics and Non-Formal Ethics of Values.* Trans. Manfred S. Frings and Roger L. Funck. Northwestern University Press, Evanston, IL, 1973.

———. *Selected Philosophical Essays.* Trans. David R. Lachterman. Northwestern University Press, Evanston, IL, 1973.

Schelling, F. W. J. *Phiosophical Inquiries into the Nature of Human Freedom.* Open Court. LaSalle, IL, 1992.

Schlanger, Jacques. "The Philosopher and His Mask." *Diogenes: The International Council for Philosophy and Humanistic Studies.* Berg Publishers, Providence, 1992.

Schopenhaur, Arthur. *The World as Will and Representation.* New York: Dover Publications, Inc., 1966.

Sciacca Federico, Michele. *Panorama del Pensamiento Contemporaneo. Vol. 1.* Ediciónes Guadarrama. Santa Catalina, 3 Madrid, 1959.

Searle, John. *Minds, Brains and Science.* Harvard University Press. Cambridge, Massachusetts. 1984.

Silver, Philip W. *Ortega as Phenomenologist: The Genesis of Meditations on Quixote.* Columbia University Press, New York, 1978.

Smith, Huston. *The Religions of Man.* HarperPerennial, New York, 1992.

Sobejano, Gonzalo. *Nietzche En España.* Biblioteca Romantica Hispanica, Madrid, 1967.

Sokolowski, Robert. "Exact Science and the World in Which We Live." *Lebenswelt und Wissenschaft in der Philosophie Edmund Husserl,* pp. 92-106. Edited by Elisabeth Stroeker. Frankfurt: Vittorio Klostermann, 1979.

Spengler, Oswald. *The Decline of the West.* Alfred A. Knopf, New York, 1962.

Stern, J. P. *Friedrich Nietzsche.* Penguin Books, New York, 1979.

Strawson, P. F. "Semantics, Logica y Ontologia" *Revista De Occidente,* Madrid, 1974.

Toynbee, Arnold. *Experiences*. Oxford University Press, New York, 1969.

Unamuno, Miguel de. *Selected Works of Miguel de Unamuno: The Private World*. Vol. 2. Princeton University Press, 1984.

———. *Un siglo de Ortega y Gasset*. Editorial Mezquita, S.A. Madrid-1 Claudio Coello, 76, 1st edition, 1984.

Valery, Paul. *Idee Fixe*. New York, Pantheon Books, 1965.

———. *Masters and Friends*. Trans. Martin Turnell. Pantheon, New York, 1968.

———. *The Outlook for Intelligence*. Trans. Denise Folliot and Jackson Mathews. Princeton University Press, Princeton, 1962.

Van Ness, Peter. "Nietzsche on Solitude: The Spiritual Discipline of the Godless," *Philosophy Today*, 32:4 (Winter 1988).

Vasari, Giorgio. *The Lives of the Artists*. Trans. Julia and Peter Bondanella. Oxford University Press, Oxford, 1992.

Walgrave, J. H. "La Filosofia de Ortega y Gasset." Trans. Luis Daal. *Revista de Occidente*, Madrid, 1960.

Warner, Rex. *The Greek Philosophers*. New American Library, New York, 1958.

Wertheimer, Roger. "Socratic Skepticism." *Metaphilosophy*. Ed. Armen T. Marsoobian. Vol. 24 no. 4 (October 1993).

Wittgenstein, Ludwig. *Tractatus Logico-Philosophicus*. Trans. D. F. Pears and B. F. McGuinness, Humanities Press, 1992.

Woolley, Leonard. *The Beginnings of Civilization*. New American Library, New York, 1965.

Zea, Leopoldo. *The Latin-American Mind*. Tran. James H. Abbott and Lowell Dunham. University of Oklahoma Press, Norman, 1963.

Zizek, Slovoj. "I or He or It (The Thing) Which Thinks." *Graduate Faculty Philosophy Journal*. Vol. 16 no. 2.

Zubiri, Xavier. *Naturaleza, Historia, Dios*. Alianza Editorial Sociedad de Estudios y Publicaciones, Madrid, 1944.

———. *Sobre La Esencia*. Sociedad de Estudios y Publicaciónes, Madrid, 1963.